LEYTE
LUZON
MANILA

. . . places where thousands of Americans **** bloody battles that finally turned the tide for America in World War II. Who was the man who led the Japanese to fight so tenaciously in the face of certain defeat, who cost the Americans such a hard-won victory?

While Manila was being razed and raped by Japanese troops, while his soldiers were dying of starvation in the hills, Tomoyuki Yamashita finally bowed to the orders of his Emperor and surrendered to American forces. Official historian Robert Ross says of the brilliant general, "No one can ever dispute the fact that Yamashita executed one of the most effective delaying actions in the whole history of warfare."

Yamashita was the first Japanese to be tried as a war criminal; as general he was held responsible for the atrocities committed by the soldiers under his command. Was his conviction in accordance with the code of American justice? Or was he a scapegoat of war, was he sent to the scaffold in vengeful retaliation for overwhelming American losses?

JOHN DEANE POTTER is a novelist, newspaper columnist, TV writer, and BBC broadcaster. He served with the British India Army and the first and second Wingate Expeditions (long-range commando units) in the Asian theater of action in World War II. While in the Philippines heading up the London Daily Express war correspondents team, he interviewed General Yamashita in the military prison near Manila. He later spoke, at length, with the general's widow, who gave him access to her husband's papers, books, and photographs.

SIGNET Books of Related Interest

The Life and Death
of a Japanese General

◎

by *John Deane Potter*

A SIGNET BOOK

Published by THE NEW AMERICAN LIBRARY

ACKNOWLEDGMENTS

For help in the preparation of this book, I owe thanks to a great many people:

First of all, to Generals Miyama, Yoshiwara, and Nisiura.

To General Sawada, Yamashita's boyhood friend; to General Manaki, his chief of staff in Malaya; to General Harada, his adviser on air operations during his mission to Germany; to General Ayabe, chief of staff in Manchuria; and to Colonels Takada and Kurihara.

Also to the Chief of Japan's Self-Defense Force, General Sugita.

To the General's widow, Mrs. Hisako Yamashita; and to Kimae Tojo, daughter of Japan's wartime premier.

To former Domei correspondents Iwamoto, Takafumi Hishikara, Matsuo Ogawa, and my old friend Kinoshita.

To another old friend and colleague, S. "Victorious Dragon" Chang, now of Time, Inc. And very special thanks and appreciation to that indefatigible organizer and charming companion, Koichi Obata.

To Captain Capotosto, of Manila, formerly of the U. S. Army in the Philippines.

Also to Robert Ross Smith, Colonel Garland, and their helpful colleagues in the office of the Chief of Military History, Department of the Army, Washington, D. C.

The author also wishes to express his thanks to the authors and publishers of the many official dispatches and books issued in Japan, the United States, and Britain, which reveal so many aspects of General Yamashita's life and campaigns. For a list of the references consulted in the preparation of this book, see the Bibliography.

CONTENTS

Acknowledgments V

1. An Interview with General Yamashita........ 11
2. A Village Far Away...................... 15
3. Mission to Hitler........................ 31
4. The Japanese Invasion................... 41
5. The Bicycle Soldiers.................... 65
6. The White Man's Fortress................ 75
7. On Guard Against the Russians............ 95
8. The Battle He Did Not Want..............101
9. The Heavenly Troops....................117
10. The Battle No One Wanted................125
11. End on Prog Mountain...................141
12. The Trial............................153

Appendixes 177

A Talk with Yamashita's Widow......177
The White Chrysanthemum.........179
Poems by Tomoyuki Yamashita.......183
Bibliography 185
Index 187

The Life and Death
of a Japanese General

CHAPTER 1

An Interview with General Yamashita

I met Japan's most famous general, Tomoyuki Yamashita, in a cool, clean cell block of the New Bilibid prison, twenty-five miles from Manila, where he was awaiting trial as a war criminal.

Dressed in a white silk shirt and high, brightly polished jackboots, he was sitting on a wooden bench outside his ten-foot cell. In the cell block were sixteen other Japanese generals and admirals, reading or writing at a long, scrubbed wooden table.

Yamashita talked to me at length about his career, from the time he left the little mountain village to when he became Japan's foremost general—a career that was to lead him to the whitewashed cell where he was sitting.

He was homely, and one could see how he got his Filipino name "Old Potato Face." But when he took off his glasses, his rugged face looked almost benign.

He waved his spectacles toward the twenty-one-page file which contained the indictment against him. Moon-faced General Muto was carefully reading the charges while we talked. Muto, the perfect staff officer, unmoved and efficient although he was also being held as a war criminal, rapidly covered sheet after sheet with notes as he read, trying to refute the allegations against his commander in chief.

What was Yamashita's own view of the charges? "Let me put it like this," he said. "My command was as big as MacArthur's or Lord Louis Mountbatten's. How could I tell if some of my soldiers misbehaved? It was impossible for any man in my position to control every action of his subordinate commanders, let alone the deeds of individual soldiers. The charges are completely new to me. If they had happened, and I had known about them, I would have punished the wrongdoers severely."

He paused to light an American cigarette, then said with resignation: "But, in war, someone always has to lose. What I am really being charged with is—losing the war." Then he added with a smile. "It could have happened to General MacArthur, you know."

We talked of the end of the war. "Japan would have lost," he said, "even if the atom bomb had not been developed. We were too weak—we started with too few resources. Of course, the bomb and the entry of Russia had a tremendous effect on our civilian population. But all it did was to end the war a little more quickly. It would have made no difference in the long run."

Yamashita readily discussed his Malayan campaign with me, drawing neat, soldierly maps of the country, with arrows showing where he had hooked behind the British forces to cut them off.

"Malaya gave me quite a lot of worry," he admitted. "Some of the soldiers from Britain and Australia fought like fine, brave men. I cannot, unfortunately, say the same thing about the Indian troops, who—well, the kindest thing to say about them is that they disappeared into the jungle when they saw us.

"What beat the British troops, I think, was our tactic of landing behind them in little ships and cutting them into small sections."

Yamashita revealed a significant piece of secret history to me. He said that after he had taken Singapore, he wanted to discuss with Tojo a plan for the invasion of Australia, and sent him a message: "Singapore, the great British bastion in the Far East, has fallen into our hands. The Allies are effectively sealed off. . . ." Instead of an advance farther west into Burma and perhaps India, his plan was to leave a strong garrison in Malaya and Burma and strike down the Pacific to the coast of Australia.

Tojo turned down the plan, making the excuse of lengthened supply lines, which would be precarious and open to enemy attack. But his real reason, apparently, was that he wanted to keep driving west to try to effect a junction with Hitler. In those days when the Axis seemed unbeatable, this meeting was probably scheduled to take place somewhere in the Punjab.

Yamashita's plan to conquer Australia was practically identical with his successful campaign in Malaya. He intended to land on each side of the major Australian cities and cut them off, first making a series of dummy landings to draw off the pitifully few Australian troops.

"Why, there were hardly enough Australians to have organized an effective resistance to the Japanese Army," Yamashita said. "All they could ever hope to do was make a guerrilla resistance in the bush.

"With even Sydney and Brisbane in my hands, it would have been comparatively simple to subdue Australia. I would never visualize occupying it entirely. It was too large. With its coastline, anyone can always land there exactly as he wants.

"But it is a long way from anywhere and I could have poured in enough troops to resist effectively any Anglo-American invasions. Although the Japanese General Staff felt my supply lines would have been too long, so would the American or British lines. They might never have been able to reach the place at all. We could have been safe there forever."

In my possession is a long, blue note engraved with the words: "The Japanese Government. One Shilling." After the surrender, stacks of these were discovered in Tokyo, ready in the event of an invasion of Australia. There were pound notes, shillings, and sixpences, all in paper money.

The government machinery for ruling Australia was also prepared. Several Japanese diplomats who had represented their government in Canberra were briefed to follow the Japanese armies into Australia and rule the country for the Emperor. One of them, whom I met later in Osaka, had been nominated as governor general.

If he seemed a little wistful about the invasion of Australia which never came off, Yamashita was philosophical, as a good Japanese should be about what he regarded as his inevitable execution. His face was unrevealing as he said to me: "My death does not matter. I know nothing except being a soldier and now I am no longer young. My usefulness to my country is over. I am too old to fight another war, so if the Americans wish to kill me, they will not be harming my country."

When I rose to leave him for the last time, Yamashita bowed politely and walked with me to the door. Several other generals were sitting in the corridor, playing a game with hundreds of counters which looked like checkers gone crazy. When I asked him what this was, he replied, blank-faced and unsmiling: "That is a typical game of ours, called Go. It is very Japanese indeed. The idea of so many counters is so you can take as much territory as you can from your opponent in the shortest time."

With that, he left me. I still do not know whether or not Yamashita had a sense of humor. I never saw him again, except in the dock.

CHAPTER 2

A Village Far Away

The village of Osugi Mura—"Great Cedar"—lies in a valley where the Yoshino River flows through the mountains of Shikoku, the smallest of Japan's four islands. Its name is derived from the ancient giant cedars which surround the village. They rise to over two hundred feet and are believed to be the tallest in Japan.

The Japanese are very proud of these trees and protect them as a national treasure. They also have a folk song about them: "The cedar is a life from olden times. It is already three thousand years old. It is a symbol of our ancient country. O great cedar, the noblest in Japan."

One winter's day there was a ripple of excitement among the women in the tiny village of Great Cedar. They came clattering down the frozen, unpaved street in their wooden sandals, pulling their kimonos tightly about them against the snow which hung frozen along the branches of the mountain pines. In spite of the cold, they twittered gaily like parakeets when they heard the news. The village doctor's wife had had a baby, another boy, whom she had called Tomoyuki.

It was November 8, 1885. Few of the villagers of that isolated mountain village had ever crossed the Inland Sea to the main island of Honshu, where, at Tokyo, reigned the sacred emperor who was descended from the Sun Goddess "in a line unbroken for ages eternal." Few of them had even ventured as far as the provincial capital, Kochi, twenty-five miles away along a rocky track through the mountains.

The village had a centuries-old calm, undisturbed by the outside world, and its people lived as their ancestors had for thousands of years.

Their life was frugal and hard, but they had no wish to change it. In winter their wooden houses, each warmed only by a handful of charcoal in a brazier, were always a little cold. But in summer, when they slid back their wooden walls and the small breezes rippled through the house and the crickets sang their happy song, they envied no one.

They tilled their rice fields, caught a few fish from the river, drank a little sake—the warm rice wine—from straw-plaited barrels, and then lay down to sleep on the *futons,* straw mattresses which were brought out of the cupboard at bedtime and laid on the floor. If they lived like that, did not offend their neighbors, and prayed to the God-Emperor in Tokyo every day, they would not be afraid to meet their ancestors when their time came.

As the doctor's youngest son roamed the tree-lined mountains near his home, he grew taller and more muscular than most Japanese. But he never went far from the ancient cedars, which always seemed to beckon him back. When he became older, he sat under the dark branches of the tallest tree and swore an oath that he would always try to make his life as great and tranquil as the tree itself. Later, when he began to write poems and essays, he signed them, with boyish bravura, "Great Cedar."

But he was not a diligent student, and his elder brother, three years his senior, often reprimanded him for playing truant from school. Tomoyuki admired his brother, a typical studious Japanese, who constantly nagged him to concentrate more on his studies. In later life, Tomoyuki was often to comment ruefully: "If I had only been cleverer or had worked harder, I would have been a doctor like my brother."

His brother had always wanted to follow their father's profession, and the old doctor was pleased that one of his sons would succeed him. Wearing straw sandals and a gray cotton kimono in the summer, and in winter a padded black kimono against the blizzards, throughout the years he had walked the rocky paths to visit his patients in the mountains. But the twentieth century was just around the corner and change was slowly coming even to the little lost Japanese village of Great Cedar. One of the first harbingers of the future was the doctor's elder son, who suddenly announced that although he still wanted to be a doctor, he did not wish to waste his life among the mountain slopes, visiting remote villages. He refused to learn the profession as his father's apprentice, but wanted instead to go to Tokyo to study and later practice there. To defy one's father is against all Japanese tradition, but the boy stood firm in spite of parental opposition to his wild scheme. When he left home on his long journey to Tokyo, he had only a hundred yen in his pocket.

The doctor confidently predicted his son's return as soon as the boy realized the foolishness of the scheme or ran out of money. But he did not come back. Helped by small sums sent secretly by his mother, he worked his way through college—a most unusual procedure at that time.

The father's eyes turned then toward young Tomoyuki. He decided it was time for the boy to stop roaming the mountains and have some proper education. The youth's mother, very proud of her descent from noblemen who had built a castle on Shikoku three hundred years before, thoroughly approved of her husband's decision to send Tomoyuki to his uncle at Kochi, where he would attend the Kainan Middle School.

This institution—the School of the Southern Sea—had been founded by a feudal clan chief to educate local samurai children in knightly discipline. The school and others like it had been taken over by the state on the orders of Emperor Meiji, who was trying to bring Japan out of its isolation and understood the need of the emergent nation for well-educated boys as future officers in the new armed services he was creating.

The headmaster, a descendant of the samurai knights of Shikoku, was noted for his skill at kenjatsu, the traditional fencing with a bamboo sword and protective mask. Drill and military training were as much a part of the school curriculum as study. The small boys were divided into companies and platoons and drilled for a least an hour every morning.

Tomoyuki Yamashita was only twelve when, for the first time, he proudly took his place on the parade ground under the watchful eye of the headmaster, who sat on horseback to watch his pupils drill. The boys wore a uniform consisting of a blue kimono with a navy-blue kilt underneath, heavy boots, and a soldier's knapsack. The older boys were given rifles, which they carried everywhere with them. All the pupils were constantly exhorted to be modest, polite, and frugal—the classic virtues of the soldier.

For two years, Tomoyuki paraded, drilled, and studied at this Spartan school. At the end of that time, his indoctrination was complete. When he came home for the summer holidays to his mountain village, he confided to his mother, with whom he had always been very close, that he wanted to be a soldier.

It was perhaps the best time in Japan's history for a boy to make such a decision. The country was gradually becoming modernized and increasing its contact with the outside world. Her army was evolving from semifeudal bands of henchmen serving the local lord into a European-style force. It was still largely officered by the old samurai families, but the shrewd liberal Emperor Meiji was beginning to throw the higher ranks open to selected candidates from the middle class.

To further this scheme, the Emperor had formed six cadet schools in Japan. At one of these, in Hiroshima, just across the Inland Sea from Shikoku Island, the fifteen-year-old Yamashita was enrolled as a cadet.

This was the time of the Boxer Uprising in China, and the commandant of the school, Colonel Katsura, kept the boys excited with reports of what was happening there. The Chinese mob had attacked public buildings and temples and the government had requested Japanese troops to help quell the rebellion. They had also asked European countries for help, and this was the first time Japanese soldiers had served on equal terms with Europeans.

When, in June, 1900, the Japanese and other foreign troops entered Peking and put down the rioting, the whole Japanese nation followed their progress. Among the troops sent to China was the 11th Regiment from Hiroshima. After the rebellion was over, they returned to the city, swaggering proudly along the streets in their black jackets and French kepis. They were splendid figures, the infantry in red trousers, the calvary in green, and the artillery in yellow. When they came to lecture the cadets on their experiences, their audience listened breathlessly.

Meanwhile, the boys of the cadet school continued their daily routine of army training and the instillation of military virtues. They slept in blankets on wooden army cots; reveille was at seven, lights out at nine. No opportunity was missed to stress the basic virtues of the Japanese warrior. The boys were constantly told that the two most important things in life were: (1) loyalty to the Emperor and their country; and (2) *Bushido*—the knightly way—as practiced by the ancient samurai warriors. Discipline was rigid and sport was unknown. The only physical recreation was the traditional bamboo fencing.

Yet, under this harsh regime, Yamashita thrived and became a big, strong youth—so strong that when he visited his parents for holidays, he used to run the twenty-five miles home, up the mountains from the provincial capital of Kochi. He did equally well in his lessons, never falling below fourth in his company class.

After three years, he was selected to go on to the Central Military Academy in Tokyo, for which Meiji had requisitioned the house of one of the great shoguns, the feudal lords who had once ruled Japan. This school was under the personal patronage of the Emperor himself, and for the first time Yamashita, the village doctor's son, observed the unique, mystical relationship which existed between the Son of Heaven and his officers.

At big maneuvers, the Emperor always insisted that the cadets sit near him in the Imperial stand, and he always attended their graduation ceremonies. When Parliament was due to reconvene on the same day as the graduation ceremony, he postponed the parliamentary opening to be with his boy cadets. After each graduation day, the boys were taken on a privileged special tour of the Imperial Palace and given tea and cakes under the benevolent eye of the Grand Chamberlain, the chief palace official.

Japan was still a remote and strange place at the beginning of the twentieth century, a Cinderella nation just catching a glimpse of the glittering coach of the Western world. Rickshas still carried doll-faced, rice-powdered geisha, wearing high, crippling wooden shoes, along the unpaved side streets of Tokyo to their assignations; and men and women all wore the traditional kimonos of their ancestors—the men in stern gray or black, the women as gaily colored as kingfishers. Western clothes were not seen in the streets unless worn by an infrequent foreigner.

But Japan, encouraged and exhorted by Emperor Meiji, was slowly awakening from her hazy dream and peeping with increasing curiosity and confidence into the world around her. Not long after Yamashita entered the military academy, she began to flex her muscles once again on the international scene and went to war with Russia. The Japanese casualties were soon very high and the cadets' course was shortened so they could be sent as reinforcements if necessary. Their classroom studies were replaced by fierce, grueling maneuvers, usually on the slopes of Mount Fujiyama.

When the Russians surrendered and Mukden was occupied by the Japanese forces, the cadets' enthusiasm for their country's glory was considerably marred by their personal disappointment at the ending of a war which deprived them of a quick chance for action. After the war, Yamashita was commissioned and posted to his local regiment, the 11th at Hiroshima, and life became very dull. He even had a little time to spend on family affairs.

His youngest sister had begun to attend the Girls' High School in Kochi and was staying with their uncle. He wrote her the typical letter of an old-fashioned Japanese elder brother: "Now that you are staying with your uncle, you must be very obedient. The most precious virtue of women is their conduct, so you must follow your aunt's instructions about etiquette and manners." He enclosed this note to his aunt: "My sister is only a country girl. She may want her own way all the time, but please see that she follows your kind instructions in everything."

Domestic matters, however, took up only a small part of his life. His new ambition was to enter the War College—Staff College—because only officers who passed through it ever attained high rank.

After several attempts he passed the War College entrance examination and began a much harder life than he had known in his years as a garrison officer. Periods of study were interspersed with rigorous training schemes that gave little chance for sleep, as they always included mock dawn attacks for which the troops had to be in position by midnight. There were few enjoyments or relaxations. Occasionally, a senior officer would invite them to a geisha party or a banquet, but this was infrequent.

During his last year or two at the War College, Yamashita was approached by many go-betweens hawking suitable marriages. Many of the offers involved the daughters of high-ranking generals. Even though he was already becoming known in Tokyo military circles as one of the most promising officers of his generation, he was still only a captain and one of these marriages might have helped his career materially. Yet this sturdy, homely, hard-working young Japanese officer revealed an obstinate streak which surprised all his friends. However tempting the offers were, implicit with money and promotion, he always rebuffed what he called "cold-blooded proposals."

Tomoyuki's only form of relaxation was to attend parties at the house of his elder brother, now a doctor in Tokyo. Another frequent visitor there was an old-style general named Nagayama. One day at his brother's house, Tomoyuki met Nagayama's eldest daughter, a tall, slim girl called Hisako. Marriage to her had no particular advantage for him, but he asked the general for her hand and the consent was gladly given.

It was a year before final examinations, so the marriage was put off until then. The day before his graduation from the War College, he married Hisako. He was thirty-two years old.

A year after the wedding Yamashita's wife went to live with her parents while the young officer served at the Japanese Embassy in Bern, as an assistant military attaché. Another young Japanese officer posted in Switzerland at the same time was Captain Hideki Tojo, one day to be Japanese premier in her greatest war.

The two young captains became very friendly. World War I had just ended, and they toured Austria and Germany together, taking photographs of each other, as so many tourists do. Language was no problem for, since the Japanese army was modeled on the Germany army, they had learned German in school. They visited the battlefields of the Western front and spent some time together in Hamburg. In broken, defeated Germany, food prices were soaring higher every day and Yamashita, who before had taken no interest in economics, walked about the city staring incredulously at the price tickets in the shop windows, which shot up by thousands of marks every day. He remarked to Tojo, "If Japan ever has to fight any nation, she must never surrender and get herself in a state like this."

After three years in Switzerland, Yamashita was posted back to Tokyo Imperial Headquarters with the rank of major. His German had improved so much during his stay in Europe that after five years in Tokyo he was offered the post of military attaché in Vienna.

He did not take his wife with him because he was involved in a serious squabble with her family about money—the last thing he cared about. One of his wife's relations had started a thermometer factory and asked him to give certain written guarantees about the business, which he had done. When he was asked to help the firm sell thermometers to the Army, he wrote some introductory letters but refused to become further involved. A short time before he was due to leave for Vienna, bailiffs arrived without warning to sell his house. The business had failed and the creditors were attempting to seize his property to implement his guarantees.

For a regular officer to have contracted such a debt, however innocently, was a disgrace and he felt he should resign his commission. Oriental families, however, always rally round on such occasions, and his elder brother advised him not to be so short-sighted but to go abroad and forget it; he would see that the family raised the money.

So Yamashita, still blaming his wife and her family for this episode which nearly ruined his career, traveled to Vienna alone. He stayed there for nearly three years and afterward claimed it was the best period of his life.

"Before Vienna, I knew little of the world outside the military life," he was fond of recalling. "There I read many books and made many good and interesting friends."

Having never forgotten his astonishment at the extreme inflation of postwar Germany, he registered as a student of economics at Vienna University. He also became involved in a European romance. His superior, Japanese Ambassador Ono, introduced him to the Japanese widow of an Austrian writer. Feeling a little homesick, he often visited her home on the outskirts of Vienna, where she served him sweet Japanese rice biscuits and red bean cakes. It was in her house that he met Kitty, the daughter of a German general. Her father was dead and she lived alone. Kitty and he soon became constant companions. There seems little doubt the friendship progressed further between the lonely young German girl and the Japanese officer who was estranged from his wife.

But his military career, which was the most important part of his life, still beckoned him. As the twenties died, he was recalled to Tokyo and promoted to colonel. His first act upon his return to Japan was to go back to his old village of Great Cedar. He visited the moss-grown family Shinto tomb by the pine trees on the edge of the rice fields, and stood for the last time under the ancient trees where he had spent his boyhood.

It was almost as though he recognized that he and his native country were about to take a decisive step forward in their joint destiny. The Japanese Army was on the verge of taking over the government and during this period, the so-called political generals, like Tojo, laid the foundations of their careers. Although his European experiences had given him an understanding of politics, Yamashita did not wish to become politically involved. He was interested only in his military career, in which he was rising more rapidly than most of his contemporaries.

He was given command of the 3rd Regiment, based in Tokyo, the key unit of the Japanese Army, and whoever was put at its head was always understood to be marked out for the highest rank. Yamashita turned out to be a much milder commanding officer than the regiment had been led to expect. But although he was mild, he had a mind of his own.

It was a time of bubbling unrest under the surface, particularly among the junior officers, who were very dissatisfied with the state of the Army. There were several opposing movements among them, and small disturbances, carefully hidden from the Japanese people and the outside world, occurring continually.

Even the crack 3rd Regiment was not immune. One of its officers was a lieutenant known as the "bomb officer" because "his head contained many dangerous thoughts." Many officers believed that he had been assigned to the regiment to test Yamashita. He began a campaign to collect money for a revolt within the Army and even had the fanatic impudence to approach his new commanding officer. The outcome could have been explosive, but to the surprise of all, Yamashita replied gently: "I may give you sympathy and aid—but not money." This was an extraordinary statement, because most regimental commanders were far too afraid of their jobs to show even the slightest sign of sympathy for a young firebrand.

At the end of 1930, because of "interference by the Army," the Japanese government fell. This was the start of the Army's open entry into power politics, which was to culminate, eleven years later, in Pearl Harbor.

In Mukden, fighting broke out between Japan and China. It was the beginning of the famous Manchuria Incident. Six months later, Manchukuo was established as a Japanese puppet state, but neither Russia nor the United States recognized it.

The army was also secretly and savagely active in Japan itself. On February 9, 1932, Army officers who were members of a superpatriotic group, The Imperial Way—*Kodo*—assassinated Finance Minister Inoue, and a month later the head of the great Mitsui commercial combine was murdered.

While these incidents hung like a dark cloud over Japan, Yamashita was appointed to one of the most important positions in the Japanese Army: Chief of Military Affairs. The appointment made him responsible for mobilization, national defense, and military expenditure. He was now fifty years old and had become known as a very eccentric character in Imperial Headquarters. Whenever he took a new job, he always moved his desk carefully so as to sit facing the Emperor's Palace. If he had no work to do, he would immediately lie back in his chair and drop off to sleep. He not only slept; he snored. If he was asked for a document, he would open his eyes at once, point to it, then nod off again. But if any important memorandum was placed on his desk, he became instantly alert and read it immediately. He also appeared to be asleep during some of the most important military lectures —much to the chagrin of the speakers.

Early one morning, he was asleep in bed when the telephone rang and a voice said, "I am the secretary to the War Minister. There are some young officers at his residence. Come at once." It was 6:20 A.M. on February 26, 1936. This proved to be one of the most dramatic days in the history of modern Japan—the day of the Young Officers' Revolt.

The reasons for the revolt were confused and complicated. The main cause was economic. Too rapid modernization had caused the economy to creak and brought on a period of inflation in which many young officers could not live on their pay. They were also concerned about the poverty of many millions of their fellow countrymen, and the nationwide corruption which they suspected was going on in business and politics. One of their major grievances was the thinly disguised white slavery which was increasing in Japan. Particularly in the poorer regions like Hokkaido, Japan's somewhat barren northern island, farmers' daughters were being sold by the thousand to big-city speculators by their near-starving families. These girls not yet in their teens, were shipped to Tokyo to be trained as geisha or prostitutes.

Many of the officers hated politicians and businessmen, whom they accused of trying to cut down the Army instead of allowing it to be strengthened, expanded, and modernized to the highest European standards. Their grievance was not only that the Army was ill equipped and deprived of money, but that big business, through bribery and a greed for profit, was turning out inferior materials for the troops.

Within the Army itself, there were many groups, joining together and separating like pieces in a kaleidoscope, but general unrest was strong in every officer under the rank of colonel. The most influential group was still the Imperial Way, which particularly hated the politicians.

This situation boiled over on the cold February night in 1936 when Yamashita was summoned out of bed. A group of young officers, led by Captain Nonaka, ordered their soldiers out of barracks at midnight and went to the house of the Premier to kill him. When he heard them coming, he hid in a chest. They killed a colonel whom they mistook for him, and also murdered several Japanese generals and politicians, including Inspector General Watanabe.

Nonaka then occupied the main Tokyo police station, in Marunouchi, opposite the great door of the Imperial Palace. He set up machine-gun posts in the street by the Palace moat and his tanks patrolled the streets of central Tokyo. Nonaka and his young officers, none of them above the rank of captain, said they wanted to protect the Emperor, Hirohito, while protesting against the state of the Army.

When messages told them of the revolt, high-ranking officers of Imperial Headquarters tumbled out of bed in their pajamas. It was a snowy morning and when Yamashita arrived at War Minister Kowashima's house, he saw many footprints in the snow.

An hour before his arrival, some officers had called to see the War Minister on "a grave matter concerning the nation." Kowashima had already heard of the assassinations. When he went into his drawing room and saw a group of tense young officers standing there, he was concerned for his life. The officers held out a piece of paper, saying that if he did not sign it, approving the reasons for their revolt, they would murder him. Their spokesman said: "We have taken these violent steps only to stop those people who are against the true meaning of our nation."

The War Minister sat down unsteadily. One of the young officers said in a loud voice "We will lead the nation in the right direction. You, as War Minister, must tell our Emperor why we have done this. Order the Army police and the Tokyo garrison commander to stop the fight between friend and friend."

Kowashima pleaded to be allowed to speak with senior officers before he could make a decision. After some consultation, they gave him permission and Yamashita was summoned. When he arrived, the War Minister was still sitting in his drawing room, holding the paper in his trembling hands. After a grim three-way argument, Kowashima agreed to see the Emperor at once. At the Palace an hour later, the Minister found that the courtiers had kept the Emperor fully informed of the revolt. The murder of his ministers had upset and angered the normally impassive Mikado. As soon as Kowashima came bowing into his presence, he inquired harshly: "What are you going to do about these officers?"

The War Minister replied soothingly: "I will try to do everything to settle this unpleasant incident and quiet the Army." The Emperor made no reply; he was in no mood for this kind of smooth talk.

He was more pleased with the fact that Imperial Headquarters had ordered out-of-town troops into Tokyo, and that Hibiya Park, in the center of the city, had begun to fill up with guns and tanks.

Traffic stopped and life was suspended as the populace waited fearfully for its capital to be ravaged by warring elements of the Army. By breakfast time, the whole of Tokyo was in a state of nervous apprehension, expecting civil war.

Meanwhile, Yamashita and several other officers of his rank were trying to stop a head-on clash between the fanatical young officers and the tough discipline-and-be-damned generals. Yamashita's group had a great deal of sympathy with the rebels' personal problems and patriotism. They were absolutely certain that if the Emperor sent a message telling the officers to return to their barracks, it would save bloodshed, as the officers would never disobey the Imperial command.

But the Emperor flatly refused to issue the order, huffily replying that he would not treat with rebels. Anguished discussions went on at both the War Ministry and the Imperial Palace for four days, while the rebels sat behind their machine guns nearby. The tanks stood ready in Hibiya Park, and Tokyo was paralyzed with fear and rumor.

Yamashita was appointed a mediator between the War Ministry and the rebel officers. He was particularly concerned that the Army might move in force against the insurgents, believing that such an attack would not only cause an irrevocable split in the Army, but destroy the military power of Japan for a long time to come.

Frightened by the revolt, most of the generals in Imperial Headquarters did not share this attitude, and finally an order was given for the Army to attack the young officers. The Tokyo garrison commander, however, agreed with Yamashita and on his own initiative withheld the attack, sending a message to Headquarters: "Are you seriously asking us to kill these comrades, these young officers, with our own hands?"

The generals, already angry with Yamashita, became further infuriated by this disobedience. In his role of go-between, Yamashita soon became suspect to both sides.

While the War Council sat in continuous session in the Palace anteroom, the Emperor in his private audience chamber wrestled over the situation with the War Minister. In view of the Tokyo garrison commander's refusal to obey orders, the ruler commanded a statement to be drafted. After several versions, he approved one that said: "We acknowledge your act was done on the basis of an idea, but the nation's future should be made clear. Everything should now be left in the heart of the Emperor."

When Yamashita delivered this statement to the rebel officers, they were, not surprisingly, dissatisfied with it. He tried to reason with them: "I am sure your demands will be put to the Emperor. If not, we will not let you die alone. Many of us must take the blame, as this has happened under our command."

When he reported back with an account of the rebels' attitude, the Emperor realized at last that there was only one course open to him—the one that originally had been suggested by Yamashita and his group. He was reluctantly forced to deal with the rebels to the extent of giving them a direct command, and signed an order which said simply: "I want to tell my soldiers to go back to their barracks."

The Son of Heaven had spoken. When they received this

message, the young officers immediately dismantled their machine-gun posts and the tanks began to trundle back to barracks. There was a great sigh of relief from the citizens of Tokyo, who had been quite convinced that their city was going to be made into a battleground. All of the officers returned with their men except Captain Nonaka, their ringleader, who shot himself as he had sworn to do if the rebellion failed.

Yamashita returned home after four days without sleep. He took off his uniform, put on a kimono, and sat with his head in his hands, muttering: "Oh, those young fools—why didn't they all commit hara-kiri? That would at least have been the end of it." He knew that once the revolt was over, there would come the vital and vexatious question of how to deal with the rebels. The War Ministry was split in two. Most senior officers wanted the severest punishment meted out to the rebellious officers. The other view, to which Yamashita was a subscriber, was that although they had taken a very impetuous and murderous way to draw attention to a great problem, their loyalty was unquestionable, and they should be treated with as much leniency as was commensurate with discipline. Eventually, a compromise was reached. Thirteen of the ringleaders were sentenced to death, but the others were only discharged with ignominy.

The whole episode haunted Yamashita, who thought that officers of his rank and importance should not have allowed such a situation to arise. Although friends advised him that, as Chief of Military Affairs, he was in command of one of the nerve centers of the whole Japanese Army and on the threshold of generalship, he wanted to resign his commission.

This was not such a quixotic attitude as it might appear. Among senior officers there was a great deal of resentment against this young colonel who appeared to have sided, if only slightly, with the rebels. It was the sort of situation that could have ruined his career, as the generals might feel he was too unorthodox to merit further promotion.

There were two very important people, however, who did not feel this way. One was the Emperor, who having recovered from his anger, recognized that Yamashita was too valuable an officer to lose. He sent the colonel a confidential message saying that he had heard of his intention to resign his commission and asking him not to be hasty. That settled his dilemma, of course; no Japanese officer would ever disobey his Emperor.

Another man, who in the future would have a long association with Yamashita, also had no wish to see him sacrifice himself. This man, General Hisaichi Terauchi, the son of a former premier, had a long talk with Yamashita about the situation. Terauchi acknowledged that the chief of Military Affairs had made many enemies by his attitude during the revolt but insisted that the situation was by no means irrevocable. He suggested that Yamashita leave Tokyo for a while until the situation had adjusted itself, and arranged for him to be posted as a major general to the Japanese-occupied territory of Korea. Yamashita took the appointment with misgivings.

Having long ago forgiven his wife, Hisako, and her family for the other situation that had nearly caused him to resign his commission, he asked her to come with him to Korea, in a way typical of a Japanese husband. He returned from the War Ministry one evening and announced: "I am going to Korea and you are coming with me. You will read all about it in tomorrow's papers." Being an obedient Japanese wife, she had never asked about the trouble over the Young Officers' Revolt, nor would he have dreamed of telling her anything about it.

Yamashita spent eighteen months in Seoul, and put all thoughts of further promotion out of his mind. He dined at home every evening, which was something new. Before this, most evenings had been spent in military duty or working late at the War Ministry. For his wife it was the happiest time of their marriage, and even he admitted: "There is a Japanese saying: 'If a man becomes a beggar for three days on end, he likes it so much that he does not want to do anything else.' That is how I felt after the quiet home life in Korea."

But the Japanese were still fighting in China, and Yamashita was soon transferred to the front as a divisional commander. Not until he received a promotion to lieutenant general was Yamashita certain that his military career would continue; he felt then that perhaps the incident of the Young Officers' Revolt might at last be forgotten.

After his promotion, the division was taken over by an old friend, General Sawada, who had marched side by side with Yamashita on the cold parade ground of the Kainan Middle School. Following the transfer of command, the two men sat and talked all night in a Manchurian inn. Yamashita confided his hopes and fears to his old school friend—a thing he would never have dreamed of doing to his wife.

"When I was posted to Korea," he told Sawada, "I felt I had been given a tactful promotion but that in fact my career was over. Even when I was given my first fighting command in North China, I still felt I had no future in the Army, so I was always in the front line where the bullets flew thickest. I sought only a place to die."

This unflinching behavior by its general had made his division the best in China.

CHAPTER 3

Mission to Hitler

In the thirties, North China was a long way from the West, and when the European war broke out in 1939, it did not appear to be of much concern to Japan. But in September, 1940, a year after the European war began, the Tripartite Pact was signed by Germany, Italy, and Japan. Yamashita's old friend Tojo, who was now War Minister, was greatly responsible for engineering closer ties with Germany and Italy; he was already scheming to enter the war.

He also persuaded the Cabinet, headed by moderate Prince Konoye, that Japan should send a military mission to Europe to find out as much as they could about the German and Italian methods of fighting a modern war. He was particularly concerned about the Japanese Air Force and wanted to have firsthand information about the bombing of Britain—how it was done, with what sort of planes, how many, and with what result.

As soon as this idea was approved, many generals proposed that Yamashita lead the mission. Tojo, jealous of rivals of his own generation, was not eager to give him the job, but the choice was so unanimous that he appointed him Inspector General of the Air Force and recalled him to Tokyo.

The suspicion and intrigue which pervaded the higher ranks of the Japanese armed services was at its height at this period.

Before Yamashita left China he heard that Tojo had not wanted to give him the job and was just waiting for him to make a mistake. Even his old school friend Sawada warned him: "If you say anything out of place to the newspapers, Tojo will make trouble."

He had his first taste of the publicity that goes with a key appointment when he arrived at Tokyo's main railroad station. Press cameras flashed and reporters tried to interview him, but he refused to make any statement. He wanted to see Tojo first. Next day, after lunching with the War Minister, he called a press conference at Air Headquarters. He spoke modestly, "As you know, I have no knowledge of aviation. As Air Force Inspector, I feel like a duck among eagles, so please treat me as gently as possible."

He then paid a great tribute to the German Air Force. "It has made a great success in the blitzkrieg because the German people have many great scientists," he said. "An air force is like a clock. The fingers move smoothly across the dial, but behind it is a complicated mechanism, a mass of scientific knowledge. In my job as head of the Japanese Air Force, I intend to take care not only of the watch face but of the more important works behind it."

This gentle, bantering speech, spiced with a few well-chosen tributes to his predecessor, mollified the suspicious Tojo, who had expected him to be much more aggressive in his utterances.

Shortly before Christmas, 1940, a party of forty experts under the command of General Yamashita left Tokyo and began to make its way across Siberia to Germany and Italy. As head of the mission to the Axis countries, Yamashita was accompanied by an Army general, an Air Force general, and an admiral, each with his own team of technical advisers. The Navy group had little to do with the other two delegations; it was customarily a separate command and resented a close liaison with the other services.

The Germans received the Japanese mission with full pomp. Yamashita's first appointment was with Hitler at the Chancellery in Berlin; he presented the Führer with messages from Tojo and a silver model of a flying crane. The meeting seemed to go off cordially. After his private interview with Hitler, Yamashita issued a high-flown statement to the German and Japanese press, which said: "I feel that Hitler's mind is spiritual, transcending material plans. The Führer told me that he has been attracted to Japan since boyhood and has promised to instruct Germans 'to bind themselves eternally to the Japanese spirit.'"

Privately his opinion was different. He told members of his staff that he considered Hitler "an unimpressive little man." He added: "He may be a great orator on a platform, with his gestures and flamboyant way of speaking, but standing behind his desk listening, he seems much more like a clerk."

In Hitler's opening statement to Yamashita, he had claimed: "All our secrets are open to you." But Yamashita reported afterward: "His promise to show all his equipment was meaningless. There were several secret pieces of information which he did not want us to know about. Whenever I tried to persuade Hitler or the German General Staff to show us certain things, like radar, about which we had a rudimentary knowledge, the conversation always turned tactfully to something else."

Hitler, on the other hand, was very anxious to obtain whatever advantage he could from Yamashita. Immediately after his promise to show all his secrets, he went on, almost without a pause, to suggest that now that Tokyo had a three-power treaty, it should hasten to declare war on Britain and America —especially America. Yamashita was fully aware of Hitler's hope that if Japan did attack America it would prevent United States interference in the European war.

Yamashita would have none of this. He told Hitler firmly: "My country is still fighting in China, and we must finish that war as soon as possible. We are also afraid that Russia may attack us in Manchuria. This is no time for us to declare war on other countries. The main aim for which we have come to your country is to inspect your armed forces and see how we can improve our own defenses."

It was on this unsatisfactory note that Field Marshals Göring and Keitel and other members of the German General Staff sat down with the Japanese leaders to plan a five-month tour of German military installations and factories. But first the Germans insisted on trying to impress the Japanese mission with the way they were winning the war. Yamashita was taken to occupied France to be shown the recently captured Maginot Line. Then Göring drove him to a château in a wood in northern France, the headquarters of

Kesselring's Air Force, from which the air attack on England was being directed.

Göring boasted to Yamashita that England would be beaten to her knees by bombing alone. "If I have to throw in my last airplane, I will gain victory," he said. "But it will not be necessary." Like Hitler, he was anxious for Japan to come into the war, and told Yamashita that if she did so before England was beaten, she would be able to share the victor's spoils when Germany and Italy split up the world between themselves.

He took him to the Pas de Calais airfields, near the French coast, to watch bombers and fighters waging war on Britain. Yamashita and his generals sat in sandbagged dugouts watching the planes take off. In spite of Göring's continual boasting, Yamashita was making his own shrewd assessment as he stood gazing over the Channel toward the English coast.

He ducked into slit trenches as the Spitfires buzzed over the French coast like angry bees, making constant sweeps, getting bolder every day. His view was that the conflict was not going at all well. The Battle of Britain had already been lost and the Germans could not cross the Channel in daylight anymore. Their night bombers were suffering losses and the crews he saw returning from raids were not in a very victorious mood. Except for the senior officers, who were all fanatical Nazis, their morale did not seem to him to be very high. His conclusion about the air war against England was exactly the reverse of Göring's claim. Yamashita thought it was already won—and not by the Germans.

This failure by Göring's *Luftwaffe*, however, did not alter Yamashita's view that the air force was still the paramount arm in modern warfare. Seeing the quantity and quality of the German and British planes, he decided that, if Japan were to go to war, she would need at least two years of intensive industrial activity to build up her air power. On the other hand, he was not overimpressed with the individual characteristics of the German planes, particularly the fighters; the Messerschmitts, for instance, could not make as tight turns as the Japanese Zeros.

What most impressed Yamashita was the high rate of production of aircraft and other war materiel. He and his generals saw assembly lines for airplanes and tanks which displayed all the German genius for efficiency. Untrained girls were operating machines which cut five pieces in one operation. This was followed by a thoroughgoing inspection, ensuring that nothing left the factories which was not perfect. Yamashita felt no doubt that Japan, with its great reservoir of unskilled female labor and a similar type of efficiency, could copy and utilize this system to great effect. He was also impressed by the unification of the three German fighting services. He felt that this amalgamation of the war effort, particularly if it applied to the Navy, would be a great asset to Japan.

As a field general, he was personally fascinated by a new German method of infantry attack, which called for a much closer coordination between infantry and artillery than was ever seen before. In dummy attacks with real weapons, he saw the infantry, armed with stick bombs and flame throwers, follow right behind a big artillery barrage to assault concrete bunkers. He was fairly certain that what he was watching was a gigantic rehearsal for an attack on Russia—and it was not long afterward that this cooperative infantry-artillery attack was used by the German infantry to overwhelm the Russian pillboxes.

After the first few weeks of their inspection tour, the three sections of the Japanese mission split up to examine factories and training systems dealing with their own special fields. When the Navy experts were impressed with a new type of German torpedo, Hitler lavishly offered it to them and ordered a German submarine to take it from Kiel to Yokosuka, the Japanese naval base. It arrived just before the attack on Pearl Harbor.

In return, Yamashita offered to give the Germans a diesel-operated tank the Japanese were perfecting. This was never delivered to the Germans because war with Russia broke out long before they could ship the engine over the Trans-Siberian railway.

Other items in the German armory that interested Yamashita were a new type of armor-piercing shell for use against tanks, and an air-cooled machine gun which fired nine hundred rounds a minute, much faster than any Japanese automatic gun.

The one weapon the Germans would not show him was radar. The Japanese who knew about it and had built a crude prototype, were convinced that the Germans had advanced much further in this field, but they could get no information. Yamashita, however, was quite equal to the German evasions.

He soon discovered that the experimental radar station was hidden in a forest near the Baltic.

One day, his air adviser, General Harada, got "lost" on a journey of inspection and, with his experts, made for the secret factory in the forest. When the Japanese drove up, no one questioned them.

It was assumed that the visit was official, and the German war factories had been ordered to throw themselves open to the Japanese generals. Harada was shown everything in the place; his experts took vital notes and carefully scrutinized every piece of apparatus. They came away with the secret of radar.

Meanwhile, Yamashita was on an entirely different kind of secret journey. He had little leisure on his fact-finding mission, but he managed to steal away to Vienna, the city where he had been so happy. He was fifty-five and his hair was graying at the temples; his staff were amused to notice that he kept a little bottle of hair dye which he used occasionally, particularly before his trip to Vienna.

He was met in the Austrian capital by the Japanese consul, then had lunch with the Japanese widow who had known him as a military attaché, and met his friend Kitty again. The only personal note in his diary of the German trip was written in Vienna: "I visited my friend the widow and in the afternoon Kitty came to see me. It was memorable."

When he returned from Vienna, his staff noticed that he now kept his hair dye in a small, green, feminine vanity case of a type not used by any Japanese woman. As he appeared to treasure it so much, it seemed obvious that it had been given to him by Kitty.

One of his last duties in Berlin was to attend a lecture given by Göring on the war situation. In the middle of it, Yamashita closed his eyes and began to snore, which sometimes occurred when he was concentrating. Göring, who was not aware of this quirk, abruptly shortened his lecture. Later, he privately complained that the head of the Japanese military mission had come to the lecture drunk.

After this final unhappy episode, Yamashita flew to Rome to meet Mussolini and his generals. He had not been there long when he received an urgent telephone call from Hitler asking him to return at once. When he arrived in Berlin, Göring told him that Germany was expecting to be attacked by Russia within the next few days and the frontier would be closed. The Japanese inspection party was to leave Germany before that happened. Göring insisted also that the Trans-Siberian railway might be closed within a day or two, marooning them in Germany. Most of the Japanese generals thought his statement ridiculous because, apart from the fact that there was a nonaggression pact between Germany and Russia, they could not believe that the Germans would give such a top-secret piece of information to a neutral foreign power, no matter how friendly.

Yamashita, however, having his own assessment of the European situation, ordered his delegation to catch the train out of Germany at once. The contingent from the Navy refused to join the party, and when Yamashita and his staff set off on the Trans-Siberian railway, seventeen members of the naval mission remained behind in Berlin. (After Yamashita arrived home, he learned that Hitler had ordered the Japanese Navy group to be taken to Argentina in a submarine. There was so little room in the vessel that they had to leave all their luggage behind—and it was still almost standing room only. After a highly unpleasant voyage which took several weeks, they eventually boarded a Japanese ship in Buenos Aires and sailed home.)

When the party neared the Polish-Russian frontier, they very quickly realized that Göring had been telling the truth, except for one particular—it was Germany that was going to attack Russia. As they approached the Russian border, they saw German armaments piled up everywhere. In every wood there were tanks, guns, bivouacked infantry, and huge dumps of ammunition and coal. No one tried to restrain the Japanese when they opened the windows to observe these gigantic war preparations. The German forces were obviously in the last stages of readiness, waiting for the order to move.

Once across the border, everything was different. Farmers were working in the fields, horses were ambling along, pulling wagons—a peaceful pastoral scene. In some places near the frontier, the Russians were hastily building antitank ditches and blockhouses behind huge canvas screens, but there were few soldiers to be seen.

Reaching Moscow, they were met at the station by General Zhukov. He invited them to the Kremlin, but they were not received by Stalin. None of the Russian officials or generals who showed them around the city and entertained them at lunch made any comment upon the war situation—or the preparations on the Polish border. And neither did Yamashita. At ten o'clock the same night, the Japanese boarded the train for the long journey through Siberia and Manchuria toward home.

Three days later, as they pulled into Irkutsk, there was a commotion. Some Italian diplomats were unceremoniously hauled off the train. Yamashita was not surprised to learn that Hitler had invaded Russia and both Italy and Germany were now at war with Stalin's forces.

The general was very perturbed by what he had seen in Europe and was convinced that the Axis nations were not doing well, particularly since Germany's invasion of Russia. He felt sure that if Japan tried to join in the war, she would imperil her own future. Stopping at Port Arthur, the terminus of his Trans-Siberian rail journey, to prepare his report, he called a meeting of members of his mission and said: "I want to talk to you very seriously. You know the results of our inspection as well as I do. I must ask you not to express opinions in favor of expanding the alliance between Japan, Germany, and Italy. Never suggest in your report that Japan should declare war on Great Britain and the United States.

"We must not and cannot rely upon the power of other nations. Japan needs more time, particularly as there may be aggression against us from Russia. We must have time totally to rebuild our defense system and adjust the whole Japanese war machine. I cannot repeat this to you often enough."

When he returned to Tokyo two weeks later, his report to the chiefs of staff caused a sensation. It suggested: (1) the unification of the Army, Air Force, and Navy; (2) the consolidation of Japan's political influence in the world; and (3) preparations on a large scale in case of a war against Russia.

He also maintained that the Japanese Air Force was much inferior in quality and size to the Western air forces, and that it should be expanded to a size at least equal to theirs. As to the Army, the medium tank should be given priority over everything else; the mechanization of all equipment should be speeded; and its manpower should be greatly increased and their training accelerated. He recommended that parachute troops be formed and their role in modern warfare be studied intensively.

Yamashita also claimed that if Japan went to war against

the United States, she very probably would have to fight Russia as well. In view of what had been seen in Europe, this was far beyond her powers. Therefore, Japan's only course was to remain patient while the Army was modernized.

The general estimated that it would take Japan at least two years to implement the military improvements he suggested. There were few generals in Imperial Headquarters who did not agree with his secret report, but there was at least one important exception—General Tojo, the War Minister.

Shortly after Yamashita returned to Tokyo, the moderate Cabinet of Prince Fumimaro Konoye dissolved. Tojo feared that he might be replaced as War Minister by Yamashita, the author of the brilliant report. This would be a major disaster to Tojo. He would have not only a powerful and popular rival overshadowing him in the political arena, but one who might postpone the war for two years and perhaps even succeed in averting it altogether. And Tojo's plans for war with the West were already well advanced.

If Yamashita had wanted to be War Minister at this stage, he had influential backing and could probably have taken over Tojo's job. But he was basically a soldier and although politically shrewd, he wanted to remain only a spectator in the political scene. "My life," he said, "is that of a soldier; I do not seek any other life unless our Emperor calls me." If he had taken a different view, considering firm opposition to war against America, there might have been a great difference in world history.

Meanwhile, Tojo was scheming to get him out of the way. While Yamashita was in Tokyo, preparing a version of his report to read to the Emperor, who had specially requested to see it, he suddenly received an unexpected order to fly to Manchuria and set up a new headquarters there.

He took the decision philosophically, noting in his diary on his last day in Tokyo: "As it was a fine day, I took my family to the sea. I had nothing to tell them except that I enjoyed having a picnic with them. About two-thirty I returned by streetcar to Tokyo."

Next day, he flew off to take up his command in Manchuria. He was not to remain there long.

CHAPTER 4

The Japanese Invasion

At the beginning of November, 1941—a month before the attack on Pearl Harbor—General Yamashita received an urgent order to leave Manchuria and report to Imperial Headquarters in Tokyo. He arrived four days later, and learned that the most crucial conference in Japan's history had taken place. Behind the high stone walls protecting the Imperial Palace in central Tokyo, Emperor Hirohito, wearing his field marshal's uniform, had presided over a small, fateful meeting.

The Cabinet had come in, bowing ceremoniously to the Emperor, who sat at the end of the straw-matted reception room. The first to make his obeisance was General Tojo, now Premier. He was followed by the chiefs of the Army, the Navy, and the Air Force, and the Finance Minister. Tojo unrolled a long piece of paper covered with Japanese characters.

The agenda, which the Emperor had seen already, and it was a simple one, was accepted in just over two hours. It contained five items:

1. War would be declared against Britain and the United States in December. By that time, the Japanese armed forces should have completed their plans and be ready for battle.

2. The first attacks would be delivered without warning,

41

and Japan's decision to enforce her Tripartite Pact with Germany and Italy would be kept secret until after the initial attacks.

3. Before the war started Japan should make a secret military alliance with Thailand to permit her troops to pass through.

4. Negotiations with the United States would be continued until the last moment.

5. If the negotiations in progress with the United States should be successful by midnight of December 1, the war plan would be called off.

The five ministers bowed and walked toward the door in their stocking feet. At the entrance, they replaced their shoes under the eye of the Grand Chamberlain, Marquis Kido, and returned to their offices to start up the machinery for war.

Next day, Japan's leading generals received their orders to report to the War Ministry. General Yamashita, still wearing his heavy Manchurian winter uniform, walked across the veranda of the two-story wooden War Ministry building to meet the Chief of Staff who gave him his orders. He was to command the 25th Japanese Army, whose main force was finishing its training on Hainan Island, off the coast of China.

Its objective was to invade Malaya without warning and capture the British naval base of Singapore, which constituted an ever-present and increasing threat to Japan's war plans in Asia and the Pacific. Ever since the outbreak of the European conflict two years before, the capture of Singapore had been part of a deliberate Japanese policy. Its conquest was to be part of a radial plan that included the seizure of Hong Kong, the Philippines, and Indonesia. When these were secured, the Japanese Army would turn south to its main objective—Australia.

The operations section of the Imperial General Staff had drafted blueprints for all these invasions. In Australia the plan was to secure the three main cities—Brisbane, Sydney, and Melbourne—in lightning attacks, after which the Australians must sue for peace, as only guerrilla activity would remain to them.

Except perhaps for the Philippines, none of these invasions could be wholly successful if Singapore remained in British hands. When Yamashita was handed the plan for Malaya, he realized his was the key role in the war.

Although the invasion plans had been approved for some

time by the General Staff, only six months earlier, Japanese officers disguised as commercial travelers were dispatched to Malaya, Hong Kong, the Philippines, and Indonesia; their task was to send back secret reports on suitable invasion points.

The officer in charge of the espionage in Malaya was Major Nakasoni. The Japanese consulates there had no inkling of his real role; he sent reports of suitable landing places directly to the War Ministry in Tokyo. His job was to measure the depth of the water, study the state of the tides and the slope of the beaches; determine whether the sand was firm enough for tank landings, and see if there were cliffs behind the beaches.

The landing places were to be in the neighborhood of the Isthmus of Kra, the narrow neck of land which joins Thailand to Malaya. After several months' exploration, he signaled coded details of three small fishing ports on the east coast. Two, Singora and Pattani, were in Thailand, about fifty miles from the Malayan border; the third was Kota Bharu, the most northerly port on the east coast of Malaya, ten miles south of the Thai border and situated at the mouth of the Kelantan River.

Major Nakasoni's first choice for a landing was Singora. It had a shelving sandy beach with flat rice fields behind it, and the harbor would provide a good anchorage. Pattani had similar terrain but Nakasoni warned that an attempted landing at Kota Bharu might be difficult because of the muddy creeks and tidal estuary. All three places shared one great asset— each of them had a good airfield nearby.

Imperial Headquarters decided to make the main landing at Singora. There would be simultaneous landings at the other two sites, but in slightly lesser strength, to confuse the British Army as to where the main thrust would develop.

While Major Nakasoni, dressed in a civilian suit, was wandering purposefully along the lonely beaches of Thailand and northern Malaya, two Japanese divisions—the 18th and the 5th—began to practice landings from steel barges in a secluded part of the Inland Sea near Hiroshima. Special officers from Tokyo supervised the landings, but a great deal of their knowledge was theoretical, for amphibious landings were comparatively rare before World War II; the Japanese were the first to employ them on a large scale.

This was the story that was unfolded to General Yamashita

in the wooden-walled room in the War Ministry in Tokyo. Both of these divisions, which would be used to spearhead the invasion, were now at Hainan Island, fully trained and ready to sail. The elite Imperial Guards would join them in time for the major drive toward Singapore. To do this, they would have to cross neutral Thailand, but the orders were that the Guards would march whether or not a pact was made with Thailand. In reserve in Indochina was a fourth division—the 56th—to be called upon when needed.

The Japanese High Command had given much thought to the constitution of these units, which were little more than half the size of the normal Japanese divisions. They had been streamlined for special landings and rapid movement through jungle and roadless territory. Since each division had been cut to 12,000 men, Yamashita had a maximum initial invasion force of 24,000 troops, and a total attacking force of 36,000 men for the assault on Singapore.

Yamashita listened to all of this with his eyes closed, as though he were sleeping. He had never seen a jungle in his life. All his overseas service had been spent in Europe or on the Asiatic mainland. His first question was about the type of troops they were giving him. He was immediately reassured. Of the two invasion divisions, the 5th was recruited mainly from Hiroshima, the nearest mainland province to his own island home in Shikoku. The 18th Division was composed of miners and farm workers from the southern island of Kyushu, one of the best sources of Japanese troops.

The military conferences on the Malayan expedition lasted for six days. Then, just a week after he had arrived in Tokyo, Yamashita was ready to take up his command of the invasion army.

He said goodbye to his wife in the Japanese Officers' Club behind the Emperor's Palace, near the Yasukuni Shrine. It was four o'clock on a rainy November afternoon, and the room where they met was cold and bare, with a floor of straw matting. Hisako, wearing her best stiff silk kimono, had come in her father's car.

Although his wife was the daughter of a general, it never occurred to Yamashita even at this moment of parting to mention a word about his new command. She sensed that he was entering upon the most important task of his career. This could only mean that war, which had been rumored for so long in Tokyo, must be imminent. Just before he left, she knelt and, lowering her head in a floor-touching bow, she murmured shyly: "I pray for your future in battle." Her husband looked at her for a moment, nodded, but made no reply. She helped him on with his shoes and he jumped into a staff car to drive to the airport.

When his plane landed at Formosa that evening a guard of honor greeted him. He inspected them, then wandered off alone into the streets to do a little shopping. The top Japanese field commander, charged with the subjugation of the white man's greatest fortress in the East, spent a few cents to buy a straw mat, to sleep on in the tropical heat.

Next day, still wearing his Manchurian winter uniform, with an orderly carrying his tropical mat, Yamashita stepped off the plane in Saigon, nerve center for the coming war with the West. He reported to Southern Region Headquarters, Japanese Imperial Army, which had been set up to direct the war in Southeast Asia and the Pacific. The supreme commander in charge of the Southern Region was Field Marshal Count Terauchi, his old chief, who had suggested his transfer from China to the present command.

Planning conferences started immediately. The most important figure at these was Admiral Ozawa, commander of the Japanese First Fleet, which was to supply the warship escort for the troop transports and close naval support for the landing operations. The Admiral and the Air Force commander agreed to give extra air and sea cover to the Kota Bharu operation—not only because the landing place was more difficult but, as this was to be the first landing in Malaya itself, they felt that the British opposition might be fierce.

The next day, Prince Takeda, who as a member of the Imperial family had direct access to Emperor Hirohito, flew to Tokyo to relay news of the plan. That night, Yamashita write in his diary:

Conference finished at four o'clock. I have a conviction of victory. It is my birthday and I always look forward to good things happening on this day. The conference finished with mutual agreement on all sides and no arguments. I am particularly glad that I have made such a detailed agreement with the Navy. We had a simple dinner with Prince Takeda to celebrate our decision before he leaves to tell the plan to our Emperor. I know I shall be able to carry out the landing plan without much trouble. I also believe we shall win, but it will cost us a great effort. I must be successful for the sake of our nation.

After three days of conferences, he felt able to relax a little, and drove with several staff officers, into the gum-tree forests of Indochina, outside Saigon. While Colonel Masanobu Tsuji, Chief of the planning staff, lectured the officers on the country, describing it as almost identical with Malaya, Yamashita wandered off into the forest alone and gazed thoughtfully at the tall, tangled trees. It was his first encounter with the jungle.

After a week in Saigon, he left for Hainan, where the main part of his army was collecting. He wrote briefly in his diary on November 25: "I left Saigon at nine o'clock in the evening and I feel at last the battle has started." Then he added a wistful revealing personal note: "I am fifty-six years old and I find I cannot write without my glasses."

In the natural harbor of Samah, in Hainan, the big invasion convoy was beginning to embark. The troops, numbering more than 20,000, carried heavy packs and wore light tropical uniforms with canvas jungle boots. Every night at dusk, half a dozen vessels came steaming into the tiny port, and the jungle-fringed harbor was alive with motorboats dashing from ship to ship.

Tanks and guns were loaded in daylight. There was no fear of discovery, because Japanese planes constantly patrolled the China Sea, watching for British aircraft and submarines. They were not only well out of range of British reconnaissance aircraft, but safe from attack—Japan and Britain were still at peace.

In Samah, Yamashita stayed at first in a hotel called The Golden Night, used by the Navy. The proprietress kept forty geisha girls, and drinking parties went on far into the night, but Yamashita never attended them. The proprietress, trying to pay him a typical Japanese compliment, sent him her daughter, dressed in her best clothes, and said: "This girl will wait on you and I have ordered her to do anything you want."

Yamashita called one of his staff and said: "Take this girl away. She is a victim. When I am going to fight against the enemy so soon, how can I take a virgin tonight?"

The next day, he went aboard his specially armored headquarters ship, the *Ryujo Maru*—"Dragon and Castle." In his tiny, airless cabin, he began to make final preparations for the invasion.

The clock ticked on, but it was still not certain that war would be declared. Then, on the evening of November 30, Yamashita was handed a coded radio signal from Tokyo. Its message was terse: "X day December 8. Proceed with plan." This meant that the landings on Malaya would start on the early morning of December 8, to synchronize with the attacks on Pearl Harbor and the Philippines.

Yamashita reached for his diary and ringed the date. He also put a blue pencil mark around January 26, 1942—the day he intended to start the attack on Singapore. He put another ring around February 11. This is Japan's National Day, celebrating the crowning of her first Emperor, Jimmu, 2,600 years before. Yamashita wanted to make a triumphal entry into the city by then.

After he received the X-day message, Yamashita did not move out of his cabin until the convoy sailed. He sat hour after hour, fingering maps of Malaya and consulting with staff officers. He was hindered by yet another aspect of Japan's administrative unpreparedness for war. The Japanese Headquarters had not supplied him with any large-scale maps of Malaya. They had none. The invader of Singapore planned his attack with maps of the type found in a school atlas. Since they did not show airfields, he had to make crosses where Major Nakasoni and other Japanese intelligence officers had pinpointed them.

He was particularly perturbed because there was not a single detailed map of Singapore available. It was not until six weeks after the first landings in Malaya that the Japanese managed to capture some military maps of the island; they found packages of them scattered in an abandoned British railway car. They were the first accurate maps of Singapore that Yamashita and his staff had seen.

While the Japanese were making these preparations for invasion, what was happening in British-ruled Malaya? The government was fully aware that the Japanese might try to take the country, not only to capture its fortress of Singapore but to control one of the richest sources of raw materials in the world. Whoever controlled Malaya had access to half the world's tin and a third of its natural rubber. It was a rich prize indeed.

On the other hand, it was not an easy place to invade. The country was as big as England and Wales but most of it was mountain and jungle, with a swampy coastline in many parts.

The British were aware of this. In 1937, a staff officer in Singapore, Arthur Percival, had drawn up details of what he considered the form a Japanese invasion of Malaya would take. His assessment of their strategy and intentions was brilliant; it hardly varied from the one the Japanese General Staff itself adopted. According to Percival's secret memorandum, which was sent to the War Office in London, the Japanese would probably attack the small port of Singora, in Thailand, because of its airfield and good anchorage. He also selected Pattani, in Thailand, and Kota Bharu, just over the Malayan frontier, as secondary simultaneous landing places.

Percival's theories were based on excellent military considerations. There was a main road from Singora which went through a small, humid Thai village called Haad'yai Junction. The railway from Bangkok also went through there, and the general who dominated this junction had an incomparable, jumping-off place from which to march south to Malaya.

The British War Office were so impressed with the report that they sent Percival back to Singapore in May, 1941— eight months before Yamashita landed—with the rank of lieutenant general, to command the British Army in Malaya.

Percival's original assessment of the situation was confirmed and consolidated by many intelligence reports he received during the months he was in command. The little jungle junction of Haad'yai had become a very busy place in the summer of 1941. Both the British and the Japanese realized that this road-and-rail junction was vital to anyone who planned to seize Malaya. The British sent what they called in their official account "officers in plain clothes," with instructions to tour Thailand and report on what they saw there.

More than thirty British officers, several of senior rank, roamed the territory in those months. They often stayed at the German-owned Zoo Hotel in Haad'yai. There, in the corridors, they ran into their Japanese counterparts, including Major Nakasoni, also in plain clothes.

The British observers reported that any invasion must come early in December because the monsoon becomes very fierce

after that and lasts until February. Once again they were
perfectly correct in their surmise. The Japanese General
Staff directed that if the attack did not begin by December
8, it should be called off, as the weather might turn it into
a catastrophe.

Armed with this brilliant counterintelligence and commanded by the man who drew it up, with every espionage
report reinforcing his judgment, the British, sitting on their
peninsula surmounted by the impregnable fortress of Singapore, should have been in a position easily to beat off the
badly supplied two-division invasion fleet which was embark-
ing from an island in the China Sea.

The British Army had in fact drawn up a plan to meet
Yamashita and his troops. Its code name was Matador. It
was to work like this: As soon as there was definite news
of Japanese invasion forces approaching, the 11th Indian
Infantry Division, stationed in North Malaya, would cross the
Thai frontier twenty-four hours ahead of their enemies and
wait for them on the beaches of Singora and Pattani.

There was, however, one drawback to Plan Matador. It
meant invading neutral territory and violating the sovereignty
of Malaya's neighbor, Thailand. This the British were loath
to do on principle. Also, they were now deeply involved in
the war in Europe, with all their big cities being shattered
by nightly German air raids. They were very anxious not to
make a mistake and take on another enemy in the Far East.
In view of these considerations, it was decided that Plan
Matador would not be employed unless the Cabinet in
London gave permission.

This was what the Japanese were banking on. They were
certain that the British would hesitate to attack a neutral
country.

Yamashita's convoy sailed from Hainan at 7 A.M. December 4. There were twenty transports, all of them under 10,000
tons, and their speed was only about nine knots. Protecting
them were two cruisers and ten destroyers, with five submarines on their flanks, ready to give warning of enemy air
reconnaissance. The 5th Division, which was to make the main
landing at Singora occupied eleven troopships, and was followed by six transports for the Pattani landing and three for
Kota Bharu.

As the vessels sailed out of the harbor, Yamashita stood
on the deck of his headquarters ship and noticed that the

sun and the moon were in the sky at the same time. He regarded this as a good omen and composed a little poem,
Japanese style, which he jotted down in the margin of his
diary.

The troop convoy's only naval escort was provided by the
submarines. The main fleet—the cruisers and destroyers—
was under orders to keep two hundred miles away from the
troopships until they were near the coast of Malaya. This was
deliberate. War had not been declared, and two separate fleets
could have been on a peaceful mission. Yamashita's convoy
could have been cargo ships or troopships with reinforcements for the Japanese forces in Indochina. The warships
could have been a strong squadron of the Japanese Navy cruis-
ing in what had become its territorial waters. But the two sailing together could add up to only one thing—invasion.

Naturally, the Japanese sailing on their secret adventure
were jittery. If they were seen, it could make a very big difference to the way the landings went.

As Yamashita sat brooding over his school-atlas maps in his
cabin, he received a signal from the fleet: "Enemy submarines operating in your area." They sailed on—there was
nothing else they could do. Actually, they did not really fear
attack, as war was still three days away. It would begin
only when they landed on the beaches.

On the same day in Singapore, one big step forward was
taken toward meeting the invasion. A telegram from Whitehall informed the commander in chief in the Far East, Air
Chief Marshal Sir Robert Brooke-Popham, that he could
operate Matador and invade Thailand without reference to the
Cabinet if he thought the circumstances justified it. It was now
a matter for his on-the-spot decision.

In addition, reconnaissance aircraft—long-range Hudsons
—had been ordered to keep a continuous watch over the
China Sea off Malaya's east coast. This sea search was to
prove fruitful. As the Japanese convoy steamed nearer
Malaya, it could no longer risk continuing unaccompanied by
a full-scale naval escort. Forty-eight hours after it had sailed
from Hainan, a rendezvous was arranged with the cruisers
and destroyers off Point Camau, the most southerly point of
Indochina.

As British warships were known to be in the area, the
convoy would have to sail in full battle formation on the

last stages toward Malaya. If they were seen by British aircraft, they would be fired upon.

They had more reason to be cautious than they knew. Two days before Yamashita sailed from Hainan, Britain had sent powerful reinforcements to her Eastern Fleet; Britain's newest battleship, the *Prince of Wales,* accompanied by H.M.S. *Repulse* and four destroyers, was anchored in Singapore Naval Base.

When Yamashita's convoy and the Japanese fleet were effecting their junction off the coast of Indochina, an event occurred which could have been disastrous for them. They were seen by two Australian reconnaissance aircraft. Yamashita signaled to Saigon: "Enemy planes shadowing our ships. They seem to have come from Borneo."

In accordance with a plan prepared for such a contingency, the invasion convoy changed course and turned into the Gulf of Thailand. This was to make the British think that Malaya was not their objective.

But would the ruse work? The planes were still on their tail. A second signal was sent to Southern Region Headquarters in Saigon: "British planes shadowing us still. Cannot know if they have sent radio signal to Singapore. If so, British will be expecting us and preparing defense line. Plan will proceed as ordered."

Shortly after the Japanese convoy turned into the Gulf of Thailand, the planes heeled away and flew westward. There was no doubt that they had reported the presence of the convoy. Whether the change of course had deceived the British would soon become known.

The Japanese could not steam in the wrong direction for too long. As soon as they were certain the planes had disappeared over the horizon, the convoy swung back on its original course toward Malaya.

What Yamashita feared had, in fact, happened. At 11:30 A.M., December 6, a Hudson reconnaissance plane reported to Singapore that it had seen warships and transports steaming westward 150 miles off the coast of Indochina. Then a second Hudson reported it had picked up the convoy.

Although the weather was cloudy and visibility poor, they were fairly accurate in their reports. The first plane reported that the convoy consisted of twenty-two ships of 10,000 tons, escorted by one battleship, five cruisers, and seven destroyers. The second plane reported a convoy of twenty-one ships escorted by two cruisers and ten destroyers. Both planes followed the force into the Gulf of Thailand, but they were nearing the limit of their range and had to return for fuel.

The two air-reconnaissance reports landed on Air Chief Marshal Brooke-Popham's desk at two o'clock that afternoon. Navigational experts estimated that if the convoy had proceeded on its original course, it would have struck Singora.

The Army commander, General Percival, was in Kuala Lumpur, consulting wtih General Sir Lewis Heath, commander of the Indian Corps in charge of the defense of Malaya. At three o'clock, he received a telephone message from Singapore telling him the news. Within fifteen minutes, he had ordered all his forces to be in a state of "first-degree readiness." The 11th Indian Division, on the northern border, was ordered to be ready at a moment's notice to cross into Thailand and implement Plan Matador.

General Percival jumped into a car and drove to Singapore. When he reached there, at 6:30 P.M., he found that further information had come in to the effect that the convoy had altered course and was steaming toward Thailand. Upon learning this, Brooke-Popham had decided to put Matador back in cold storage. "There should be no undue alarm," he stated, "because the Japanese expedition is directed against Thailand."

The troops were told to stand down. The Japanese bluff had worked. It was the first of many bluffs that Yamashita was to use in this campaign—all of which succeeded.

Yamashita had another piece of luck at this time—the weather, on the verge of the big monsoon, was turning very murky. More British reconnaissance planes, several Hudsons and a Catalina, were sent off to find the convoy. They cross-quartered the sea only a few hundred feet above the water.

The Catalina suddenly came upon the Japanese fleet through a rift in the clouds. Immediately, the cruisers and destroyers opened fire and the plane was shot down. The convoy steamed on. It was the first act of war.

In the misty, rough weather, no other aircraft picked up the invasion fleet. British troops continued their routine tasks, with the High Command convinced that the Japanese had gone to Thailand.

Their illusions were rudely shattered the next evening— December 7—when just before dusk, a low-flying Hudson suddenly caught sight of four Japanese vessels that looked like destroyers sailing seventy miles off Singora. About the same time, another Hudson spotted some Japanese cruisers. This was the first that had been seen of the Japanese convoy for thirty hours.

As soon as the Hudson reported to Singapore, there was a scurry of hurried conferences. At ten-thirty Brooke-Popham decided at last to put Matador into full operation. It was too late.

Two hours later, while orders were still going out to the troops to advance to the Thai border, there came a telephone message saying that Japanese battleships were shelling the beach defenses at Kota Bharu.

When this happened, the 11th Indian Division, which under the Matador plan was supposed to march rapidly into Thailand, was still in its original position. Not one Indian or British soldier had been moved to meet the invasion.

But Yamashita was also having his problems. The Thais were proving strangely uncooperative. A radio signal told him that they were still refusing to allow Japanese troops to proceed through their territory. He was ordered to continue the landings just the same.

This meant, however, that he would probably have to fight his way ashore in the two landings in Thailand. It would also mean that the Imperial Guards, who had to pass through Thailand to join him, might be held up.

It was just after midnight when the transports began to drop anchor off Singora. The sea was very high, with four-to six-foot waves. As the troops struggled to lower their landing craft into the rough water, Yamashita peered through the darkness toward the beach. He was looking for a secret guide light. The day before, a top-priority cipher signal had been sent to Major Nakasoni, who was staying at the Japanese Consulate at Singora. His orders were to appear at midnight on the beach, shining a lantern to show that all was well and guide them to the correct landing spots in the darkness. When Yamashita's ships anchored, the only light the troops could see came from the Singora lighthouse. When no signal appeared, it was decided to land without the guide light.

In fact, Major Nakasoni never did appear on the beach. On the night of the landing, there was a party at the Japanese Consulate, presumably to celebrate the imminent outbreak of war, and most of the Japanese officials were drunk. When the cipher signal arrived, it either did not reach the major or he was in no condition to appreciate its significance. The landings went on without his assistance.

It was shortly after midnight when a high wave tossed the first landing barge onto the dark beach. The Japanese troops waded ashore and began to run up the sand. They met no resistance until they climbed from the beach onto the rice fields, where a patrol of Thai troops fired on them.

The first battle for Malaya had begun. It did not last very long. Several other Thai patrols came up, but as barge after barge landed, they fired a few desultory shots and scattered into the darkness. The Japanese moved toward the town, occasionally encountering rifle shots from small parties of the Thai Army.

Except for these intermittent bursts of rifle fire, the little port of Singora was quiet and deserted. The temples still had their strings of electric fairy lights shining brightly in the darkness. The Japanese troops skirted them, fearing they would be an excellent target for a British air attack.

The sporadic but determined resistance by the Thai forces surprised and angered Yamashita. At 5:20 A.M., he climbed into a motorboat and followed his troops ashore. The Japanese had entered the town and made their headquarters in the social club. Half an hour later, they stormed the local police station and half a dozen policemen surrendered. But the Thai Army was still fighting.

Yamashita used the captured police station as a headquarters. At eleven o'clock, he was just about to send a signal to the Navy, standing off-shore, to open fire and destroy the little port, when a colonel of the Thai forces came in, saluted smartly, and said: "The Thai nation has decided to share its fate with Japan." A Thai-Japanese pact had been signed, which meant Japanese forces could now move freely through Thailand.

When the fighting ceased, the 5th Division had a roll call and found that nine men had been killed, including three officers, and seventeen wounded in the Singora landing.

Yamashita walked to a little hill near the lighthouse and looked out to sea. The coastline was filled with Japanese warships and submarines, and transports were landing successive waves of support troops with their supplies. He sat down and ate some cold rice from a square tin while four radio messages were brought to him.

The first was from Imperial Headquarters in Tokyo, and

stated that not only had Malaya been invaded, but at the same time Pearl Harbor, the Philippines, and Hong Kong had been attacked by Japanese forces. The second message informed him that the Imperial Guards, his third division, had arrived near Bangkok and were on the march to join him in the attack. The third said that the Pattani landings had been unopposed and successful.

The fourth message was not so pleasant. The 18th Division, landing at Kota Bharu, in Malaya, had run into stiff resistance and at least one transport had been sunk by R.A.F. planes.

The Indian troops at Kota Bharu, manning the beaches at the mouth of the Kelantan River, gave Singapore the first news of the Japanese invasion. The coast was studded with concrete pillboxes, a thousand yards apart, protected by tangles of entwined barbed wire and mines. Each pillbox was manned by an N.C.O. and six men of an Indian regiment of Dogras.

These small beach-defense units, gazing through the darkness and slashing rain, suddenly saw the shadow of great ships approaching and heard the rattle of anchor chains and the echoes of orders. They had one eighteen-pounder gun of World War I vintage, and immediately opened fire with it. At once the air reverberated with flashes and explosions from the sea as the Japanese warships shelled the pillboxes and the nearby town.

One of Major Nakasoni's subordinates suddenly shone a light from a hillside to guide the invasion fleet in. In half an hour, the first Japanese armored assault barges slid onto the beaches and palm-fringed, muddy creeks of the Kelantan River. As the mud-splashed invaders slithered up the beach in the darkness and driving rain, the pillboxes opened fire on them. The main landing was in front of pillboxes No. 13 and 14, which opened fire with rifles and machine guns. The Japanese fell back, cowering in the mud, but soon crept forward again. Twenty minutes later, there was a flash of hand grenades and the two pillboxes were captured. All the Dogras died where they stood.

Confused fighting for the pillboxes went on all night. Two companies of the Frontier Force Regiment, with antitank guns, came up in an attempt to drive the Japanese back into the sea, but by this time the invaders had hundreds of men ashore and had captured several more pillboxes. Floundering through the waterlogged fields and muddy creeks near Sausage Island, the Indian troops could not get within two hundred yards of the nearest captured pillbox. During one of these attacks, one company commander was killed.

In the misty dawn the Japanese transports and landing barges could be seen standing a few hundred yards off the mouth of the river. As soon as it was light, Hudson aircraft began to attack them and one ship was quickly set on fire. But troops from the transports were still pouring steadily onto the beaches and had begun to fight their way toward the airfield, a mile and a half away.

The Japanese were taking heavy casualties, some of the heaviest in the campaign. They discovered one unexpected hazard: slimy seaweed choking the creeks was very difficult to climb over and many men were machine-gunned as they crawled across it.

More British reinforcements, including the Hyderabad Regiment, were coming by train to join in the fighting. Before they arrived the British forces on the beach were compelled to retreat toward the airfield.

That afternoon witnessed the first of those unhappy episodes which were to plague the British until the fall of Singapore. The Air Officer Commanding in Singapore received a report that the Kota Bharu airport was under small-arms fire from Japanese ground forces. He immediately ordered the withdrawal of all planes and ground staff. When Brigadier Key, commanding the Indian brigade, arrived at the airfield to check this report, he found the Japanese were still fighting their way out of the muddy creeks over a mile away. Yet not only had all the planes disappeared and the Australian ground staff vanished, but they had left in such a hurry that the gasoline and bomb dumps and the runway were still intact. Hastily the brigadier ordered up field guns to destroy them.

The Hyderabad infantry regiment arrived at the airfield while this was going on and were put in position to resist the Japanese attack. They were not good troops, and had been openly mutinous for some time. When the Japanese attacked the perimeter, the Hyderabad commanding officer and adjutant were killed in the first few minutes of the battle. After this, according to the official accounts, "the battalion disintegrated." The remaining Indian troops began to fall back, and soon the Japanese had their first Malayan airfield. Within an hour, their own planes began to land on the still-undamaged runway.

Following the loss of Kota Bharu airfield and the hurried exit of the Australian Air Force, a state of panic overcame the retreating troops. Among the many alarming and untrue reports that circulated among the British forces was one that Brigadier Key and his staff had been either killed or captured.

During the night of the Japanese landings, the High Command in Singapore was left in no doubt as to the enemy intentions. At 4:30 A.M., the city had its first air-raid alarm when Japanese aircraft based on Indochina, seven hundred miles away, bombed Seletar and Tengah airfields and the naval base, but did only slight damage to the city. Later that morning, just as Yamashita's troops were approaching the perimeter of Kota Bharu airfield and his other division was beginning to move south toward the borders of Malaya, Sir Robert Brooke-Popham issued a statement: "We are confident. Our defenses are strong and efficient and our preparations are made and tested."

Nothing could have been further from the truth. Within the next twenty-four hours, the Japanese made great use of the three airfields they had captured. Yamashita's airmen were already so confident that within a short time of his landing a hundred Japanese aircraft were parked on Singora airfield with hardly any ack-ack protection. R.A.F. bombers attacked the field, but they had no fighter support and lost five planes out of the eleven in the squadron.

The airfield at Alor Star, on the west coast, almost parallel with Kota Bharu, was so heavily bombed that it was evacuated a few hours later. Penang, lower down the west coast, was bombed by seventy Japanese planes in its first big raid.

General Percival realized the seriousness of the situation when he wrote: "Within twenty-four hours of the campaign, the Japanese gained their first objective, but at considerable cost. Forces landed at the Kelantan River consist of rather less than one Japanese division."

Actually, however, not only was the main invasion army ashore, but most of the 5th and 18th Divisions were already driving south. It was Yamashita's task to get them moving as quickly as possible before the British, reeling under his surprise blow, recovered from the shock. He gave orders that both divisions should start south at once. The 18th, which had had such hard fighting at Kota Bharu, had no time to bury its dead, who were left lying on the beaches and around the perimeter of the airfield. Whenever possible, a finger was cut off each body and buried as a token according to Japanese custom. Then the division began its march on Malaya.

While Yamashita was sitting in the Singora police station, planning the Japanese advance, he received an apologetic visitor. It was Major Nakasoni. The major expressed his deep regret that his six-month secret survey work should have ended like this. General Yamashita's reply is not recorded.

Yamashita noted in his diary after the fall of Kota Bharu airfield: "In spite of heavy fighting, my troops are in good spirits and are successful. The Imperial Army should be proud of them."

However, the battle was by no means won. R.A.F. planes bombed the beaches at Singora while the barges were unloading and heavy equipment and supplies waiting to be transported inland were lying in great heaps. Australian Hudsons did great damage, leaving many Japanese dead and wounded among the burst bags of rice, the battered trucks, and the exploding, blazing ammunition.

Yet on that morning at Singora something else happened on the beach which was more upsetting to Yamashita than the R.A.F. attack. A large, self-propelled landing barge that had chugged within thirty yards of the beach suddenly turned around and went out to sea. It contained thirty men and two officers. No one could understand what had happened. Japanese troops, staggering under their heavy loads, turned and gaped at it until it disappeared over the horizon.

It was several weeks before the *kempetai*—the Japanese Military Police—tracked it down. It was beached on an island four hundred miles away on the other side of the Gulf of Thailand. The men aboard it admitted they had planned to desert in the face of the enemy and had secretly stocked up enough rice and fuel for their long voyage.

Yamashita wanted to bring them back to Malaya for a summary court-martial, which would probably have meant the firing squad for calculated cowardice. Instead, the two officers—a doctor and a paymaster—and their men were tried in Saigon. The officers were sentenced to fifteen years; three sergeants and other noncommissioned officers who voyaged with them in the barge received shorter sentences.

After two days' fighting and the capture of Kota Bharu airfield, the forward troops of the 18th Division needed to be regrouped. On the other hand, the 5th Division, in Thailand, was fresh and ashore in great strength. Surprise being his greatest asset. Yamashita forced them on as quickly as possible. He was afraid that his comparatively small force of 20,000 men might at any time come up against a British army of three times its number if he gave the enemy a chance to rally.

As he sent the 5th Division racing toward the Malayan frontier, the British at last decided to move. A truncated form of Plan Matador was put into operation, but like everything else in the British defense of Malaya, the forces were too few and it was too late.

More than twelve hours after Yamashita's troops had landed, the first British soldiers crossed the Thai border. They hoped that, at worst, the Thais would preserve a sullen neutrality. Instead, having just made a pact with Yamashita's forces, they resisted. The British troops ran into several roadblocks and were constantly fired upon by snipers in trees. By nightfall, they had advanced only three miles.

Four hours behind them, a formation of the Punjab Regiment crossed the Thai frontier, making for Singora with orders to harass and delay the Japanese. By dusk, they were camped outside Sadao, ten miles inside Thailand.

But Yamashita's 5th Division, driving southward, was moving much faster. When the British forces were camped at Sadao that evening, they heard the hum of approaching vehicles and saw scores of flashing headlights twinkling in the rain. Soon a column of vehicles headed by tanks appeared on the road.

The Punjabi gunners held their fire until the first tank was a hundred yards away. Three tanks were hit and the infantry-laden trucks behind them skidded to a halt. The Japanese infantrymen jumped down and fanned out into the wet jungle. There was a confused skirmish among the trees at night and the Indians, heavily outnumbered, withdrew.

The second section of Yamashita's troops, who had landed at Pattani, were also on the move. They came down a track that the British had ruled out as impossible for wheeled traffic. By manhandling their vehicles over the worst part of the muddy jungle trail, they pressed on rapidly.

The British in Singapore were already beginning to realize the type of enemy they were up against. General Percival, studying the reports of the early battles, commented: "The

Japanese infantry are showing themselves resourceful and masters of infiltration tactics. They are attacking in the traditional Japanese manner without regard for loss."

Forty-eight hours after his first invasion barges had slid onto the beach, Yamashita had an enormous piece of luck. The Japanese Navy scored an important victory. As soon as the news of the Japanese landings was received, the two great British battleships, the *Prince of Wales* and the *Repulse,* that had docked at Singapore a week before steamed northward up the Malayan coast to intercept the Japanese warships and transports. The fleet was shadowed from the start by enemy submarines and aircraft. At midday on December 10, the Japanese Air Force swooped. Four high-flying bomber squadrons attacked the warships and were followed by seven low-level torpedo squadrons, who pressed home their attack with fanatical determination.

The battle did not last very long. In less than two hours, the *Repulse* sank and the *Prince of Wales,* riddled with Japanese torpedoes, keeled over and exploded.

Oddly enough, on this day, which did more to clinch his victory in Malaya than anything else, Yamashita only commented laconically to his staff: "The Navy have done their duty. The Army must not be behind them."

This rather grudging tribute was probably due to the age-old rivalry between the Japanese Navy and Army, which were completely separate commands and jealous of each other. They applauded each other's victories, but there was no love lost between them.

Even before the destruction of the British fleet, the pattern of Yamashita's advance had been settled. Brushing aside the small, ill-organized, hastily collected British formations which tried to stop him, he followed the system Hitler's shock troops used in France. His army moved fast, carrying only ammunition and enough rice for two days. Supply trucks were sometimes a hundred miles behind, but it did not matter. The troops lived off the villages they passed.

But Yamashita's most amazing piece of audacity was the way he spearheaded his advance. First along the roads went a company armed with rifles and grenades and mounted on bicycles that had been brought along in the holds of the troop transports. This unit was followed by several tanks and truckloads of infantryman.

Though usually the Japanese cycled along for hours without meeting any British troops, if they were fired upon by the enemy, they jumped into the ditches at the side of the road and let the tanks following them go through. The British forces would report that they had been attacked by an enormous tank force. They became convinced that the Japanese had landed a great number of tanks in Malaya for this reason: tire punctures due to the tropical heat became so numerous that the Japanese finally elected to ride on the rims, making a clatter along the Malayan roads that sounded like a huge force of tanks to the defending British.

As the British and Indian troops withdrew in confusion before this bicycle-tank attack, Yamashita's troops began to equip themselves rapidly with trucks, carriers, rifles, and machine guns that had been left behind by the British in their hurried retreat. The trucks were especially welcome because the Japanese had very few in their ill-equipped expedition. There had been little room for them in the small, three-thousand-ton transports. The vehicles they did land were slow and unserviceable. As soon as they could, the fighting troops left them on the roadside and drove on in captured British trucks. Very soon, they were almost completely equipped with enemy vehicles.

While the British ran, Yamashita chased them as fast as he could, ignoring supplies and communications and all the appurtenances of the modern army, as he relied equally on weak British resistance and the staying power of his infantry.

Yamashita had several problems that had nothing to do with the British. One of his major preoccupations was the behavior of his own troops. Excited by their easy victories they were getting out of hand, maltreating the inhabitants of Malay villages from which they seized food or other supplies. When Yamashita heard about this, he had several conferences with Colonel Watanabe, chief of the political section of the Army, and insisted he take strong measures against any soldier who was found misbehaving.

He made several notes in his diary about their behavior. One entry said: "I want my troops to behave with dignity, but most of them do not seem to have the ability to do so. This is very important now that Japan is taking her place in the world. These men must be educated up to their new role in foreign countries."

But in their headlong victorious rush, no one did anything about the situation—the wishes of their commander had no effect on the junior officers and men. This was to prove to be a fatal weakness of the Japanese Army.

Yamashita was also having trouble with his communications, which were rudimentary and kept breaking down. One day, he noted in his diary: "After worshiping and paying homage to the Emperor, I went to headquarters to try and put our communications in order. I find I cannot do anything with them."

His greatest problem was to come from the most unexpected source. The advance party of the Imperial Guards began to arrive by rail from Thailand to join his two divisions. The Imperial Guards were picked troops, and their officers, who came of samurai background, tended to be egotistical and exceedingly arrogant. They did not like mixing with other officers and insisted on running their divisions in their own way, even to plans of attack.

Major General Imaye, the chief of staff, who had been a lecturer at the War College in Tokyo, was even more difficult than his divisional commander, Lieutenant General Takumo Nishimura. Imaye felt that since he had taught so many generals, he knew better than all of them. He and Nishimura were to prove so petulant that toward the end of the campaign they almost endangered Yamashita's attack on Singapore.

The Imperial Guards themselves fought well and the troops were very popular with the rest of the Japanese Army. One of them wrote a sad-boastful song called "I Will Return Home Carrying the Ashes of my Comrades," which became a great wartime favorite in Japan.

Meanwhile, Yamashita's initial attacks were going better than he had planned. He looked at his little ringed calendar several times as the reports of swift advances were brought to him. His bicycle troops and infantry in British trucks, using small mortars and infantry guns when they met the enemy, were making thirty miles a day.

Attacked by these columns, which included a handful of fast-moving light tanks, and constantly bombed and machine-gunned from the air, the British were beginning to crumble. Penang, one of Malaya's biggest European settlements, which had been under bombing attack constantly, was evacuated eight days after the Japanese landings.

In addition, the British were having very serious troop trouble. The Indian forces were dismayed and angry to find the British Empire, which they had always regarded as glorious and victorious, outclassed in tanks and airplanes— the two essentials of modern warfare. As they tried to form a line to defend southern Malaya, the Indian morale was very low.

On the other hand, the spirits of the Japanese were soaring. Hardly a fortnight after his invasion, Yamashita had taken all of Malaya above the Perak River, including the island of Penang. What was equally important, the Thai railway line had been repaired and three abandoned trains captured at Singora. The Japanese self-propelled landing barges were loaded on them and sent by rail from Singora across the narrow waist of the peninsula to Alor Star, on the west coast of Malaya.

From there, a good railway track ran southward to Singapore.

CHAPTER 5

The Bicycle Soldiers

The fateful year of 1941 was nearly over. The British High Command had not proved successful, and various drastic changes were being made. Air Chief Marshal Brooke-Popham, neither a successful nor a decisive commander, was relieved of his post. He was sixty-two and Whitehall still persisted in the story that this was "a routine posting" which had been decided upon before war broke out. General Sir Archibald Wavell—later Field Marshal Earl Wavell—was made Supreme Allied Commander in the Southwest Pacific, with headquarters in Java.

These British moves were far too late. On New Year's Eve, Yamashita was implementing a plan which was to hasten considerably the fall of Singapore.

He had with him forty large and small boats, used in the Singora landings, which had been brought by rail to Alor Star. He also had portable motorboats, capable of being carried through jungles and assembled on beaches and river-banks. This small flotilla could carry more than a battalion of infantry, a section of mountain guns, and a section of engineers.

Yamashita decided to put fifteen hundred men of the 5th Division into the boats and land them behind the British lines, to throw them into further disorder. The Japanese set off on

New Year's Eve. On the day after he took this gamble, the general felt confident enough to write in his diary:

> On this first day of the new year, I breathe the air of the South. I was up at 5 A.M., and it was already hot.
>
> I must put away recollections of the past. My duty is half done, although success is still a problem. The future of my country is now as safe as if we were based on a great mountain. However, I would like to achieve my plan without killing too many of the enemy.

His staff, however, were not so optimistic. At 25th Army Headquarters, nearly all his officers opposed the landings as too dangerous. The flotilla was an easy target for annihilation by the British Navy patrolling the coast.

Yamashita's planning officer, Colonel Tsuji, particularly disapproved of the idea. The 5th Division was moving very fast along the main road, with the mountains on one side and swampy jungle on the other. Tsuji's view was that they had very successfully crashed through all British road barriers, ambushes, and other opposition, so that a coastal landing was unnecessary. Not only did he fear the risk of losing troops but also he was concerned about the potential loss of barges, which must be kept to cross the Johore Strait when they reached Singapore.

Yamashita overruled Tsuji and ordered the fifteen hundred men, commanded by a colonel, to land south of the British forces. But the fears of the high-ranking Army officers had communicated themselves to the officers on the expedition. The voyage was scheduled to take nearly a week. But when, after four days at sea, an R.A.F. plane flew over his ships, the colonel landed in a river mouth well north of his objective.

Only one unit, of one hundred men, landed at the right point. They became separated from the main flotilla and reached their landing place without air attack. When they found no one else there, they sailed back along the coast to rejoin the Japanese main forces.

Unaware of the failure of the landing plan, the British saw dozens of barges approaching a small village at the mouth of a river. Their twenty-five pounder guns sank one of the barges, but the Japanese colonel managed to get most of his troops ashore. They landed among the mangrove swamps and disappeared into the thick jungle.

The Japanese force was literally floundering about on the coast of Malaya, but British Headquarters saw it as a new and frightening development and made hurried plans for further evacuations.

Meanwhile, the rest of the 5th Division was driving along the road near the federal capital of Kuala Lumpur. Parallel to the road, separated by four hundred yards of dense jungle, ran the railway.

To defend Kuala Lumpur, the British decided to stand on the Slim River. They did not blow up the concrete bridge over the river, but placed explosives ready for its demolition in case they had to abandon it.

Japanese aircraft flew up and down the road and railway, bombing and machine-gunning. Then they attacked in two waves: small motorboats, which they had manhandled through the jungle, began to cross the river, while tanks advanced in a frontal attack along the road where the British had laid concrete cylinders.

A British 4.5 howitzer, half hidden behind the blocks, waited until the leading tank was twenty-five yards away before opening fire. The tank shuddered, stopped, and burst into flames. As the commander and his crew tried to climb out, they were machine-gunned. Other tanks piled up behind it, but the Japanese infantry quickly fanned out into the tangled jungle and attacked along each side of the road. They cleared a way for their tanks, which began to rumble slowly toward the bridge.

Although British twenty-five pounders covered the road, ten Japanese tanks forced their way onto the bridge and an officer with a saber cut the wires leading to the demolition charges. The bridge was captured intact.

The Japanese infantry, however, were still held back by the British and could not cross. The tanks pressed on and at nightfall they were cut off from their own troops most of whom were still on the opposite bank.

Then, in bright moonlight, the jungle became alive with guns firing, men yelling, and even cans clattering. The Japanese were making a full-scale attack to join up with their armor.

After nineteen hours, the battle was over. Not only had the Japanese freed their tanks, but they had crushed all

British resistance and begun to advance rapidly along the road again. The British were thrown into such disorder that no one sent a message to inform the rear of the major Japanese breakthrough.

Japanese bicycles, tanks, and truckloads of infantry began to roll down the road so fast that they were ten miles behind the British lines before anyone realized it. The first to encounter them were two British infantry battalions and an artillery unit, marching along the road to join the Slim River battle. Japanese tanks ran straight through them, firing, and massacred the forward troops before the rest fled into the jungle.

The Japanese captured 54 guns, 50 armored cars, and 550 vehicles abandoned by the fleeing British troops. More than 1,200 prisoners surrendered on the banks of the Slim River, and 2,000 more came out of the jungle, half-starved, to give themselves up during the next three days. Enough food and other supplies were captured to keep Yamashita's whole army going for a month.

The day the Japanese forced their way across the Slim River, the 11th Indian Division, charged with the defense of North Malaya, ceased to exist as a fighting formation. The battle also sealed the fate of Kuala Lumpur. The British decided to give it up.

This decision was reinforced by the British encounter with the battalion of Japanese who had landed down the coast in the wrong place. It seemed to them that large forces of enemy troops were now roaming in their rear.

On the Japanese side, there were still mixed feelings about the landings. Colonel Tsuji felt he had been proved right because the 5th Division had broken through along the road without any help from the landing party. He was also depressed because after the battle he had to deliver an unpleasant message to an old Military College friend who had commanded a front-line battalion at the Slim River. Yamashita had sentenced the latter to thirty days' close arrest because three of his men had looted and committed rape during the advance. Referring to this episode and others like it Yamashita noted in his diary:

We still have many things to do among ourselves. Our education and outlook are not what they should be. We must encourage the sort of outlook that will make us proud of our nation. Those who have come to Malaya without this outlook may be debased. This is one of the things I must keep a careful watch over.

Yet this is one of the few recorded instances in which Yamashita took firm disciplinary measures against the sort of behavior which was to bedevil him throughout his fighting career. His own behavior was impeccable, but he seemed to be completely ineffectual in preventing and punishing such acts among his troops.

After the Slim River battle, he came across three British prisoners of war. He stopped his car and, through an interpreter, asked about their homes and families. Then he turned to the Japanese guarding them and said: "Do not despise these men. After fighting bravely, they have been unfortunate enough to be captured. Treat them kindly." How little his officers and men obeyed his exhortation to kindness was demonstrated in later battles in Malaya.

The coastal landings had been a partial failure. Should he discontinue them, as most of his staff, led by Colonel Tsuji, advised? He made up his mind to carry on with them, but to make a switch in his dispositions.

Although the 5th Division had been specially trained at Hiroshima and Hainan for landings, they had not proved themselves very resolute when faced with even small enemy sea or air attacks. He made up his mind to use the Imperial Guards in their place. They had had no training for landings, but they were crack troops who could be trusted to carry through any unusual attack.

When he heard he had been overruled, Colonel Tsuji became so angry that for forty-eight hours he refused to speak to anyone or take part in the war. This temperamental behavior, which Imperial Guards commander General Nishimura was to exhibit constantly, was apparently not uncommon among high-ranking Japanese officers.

In spite of the colonel's sulks, the landings proved to be one of Yamashita's most successful moves. His hooks down the coast behind the British lines were so unorthodox and upsetting to the conventionally trained British officers that they began to retreat twice as fast. And the Imperial Guards fulfilled their role with reckless daring, landing in the most inhospitable swampy jungles behind the enemy lines—in the Japanese phrase, "Like a blind man who does not fear snakes."

Yamashita made an even bolder decision at this time. He decided the campaign was going so well that he did not need the 56th Division, which was held in reserve. He signaled to Saigon that they could send it to help the invasion troops in Burma. This decision was based on several factors. He was beginning to run short of food and ammunition, and he realized that at Singapore he would have to attack on a narrow front and another 10,000 men might be more nuisance than they were worth. But there is little doubt that the real basis of his action was a growing contempt for his enemy.

The British were still fleeing fast, accompanied by all the panic, uncertainty, and confusion which a major retreat brings with it. The single-track railway line down the coast from Kuala Lumpur to Singapore became so clogged with traffic that thirteen trains were shunted onto the siding and left there. When it was realized they were still undamaged and contained material useful to the Japanese, R.A.F. planes were ordered to machine-gun and bomb them. These forays were not successful and many of the trains remained intact. One of them contained hundreds of detailed maps of Singapore Island, just printed by Malayan Survey at Kuala Lumpur to be ready for the defense of the city. These were captured by Yamashita's troops. So that when the battle for the fortress began, the Japanese officers were fully equipped with brand-new maps of Singapore, while the British had none.

Yamashita began to prepare for the last big drive toward Singapore. He knew it would have to be a two-pronged attack, along both coasts.

The British were also aware that the big battle for Singapore was impending. After the Slim River disaster, they decided to withdraw to Johore, the Malayan state adjoining Singapore Island. They also drew up plans for the destruction of the Johore Causeway, preparatory to pulling all their troops into Singapore for a last stand.

The last remaining natural obstacle before Yamashita was the Muar River, spanned by a trunk road and a railway bridge. It was six hundred yards wide and surrounded by low-lying swampy country. Once across it, the rest of the country consisted mostly of rubber plantations and cultivated rice fields, which made easy going all the way to the Johore Strait.

On January 18, British intelligence reported two Japanese divisions coming down the main road toward the banks of the Muar. The British information was quite correct. Driving as fast as their leading cyclists could pedal were the 5th Division and the Imperial Guards. Australian and Indian troops, waiting for them, had felled trees across the jungle tracks and placed concrete obstacles on the main road to hold them up.

To finish the battle, Yamashita decided to make his biggest landing. While the main force of the Imperial Guards led the attack down the road, he detached a brigade to land behind the Australian lines. When the Australian soldiers saw Japanese troops on the opposite bank of the Muar River, no one bothered to send to the main British forces a warning that Yamashita's troops were mustering in force on the river bank—another of those inexplicable acts of omission which dogged the British side of the Malayan campaign.

In the middle of the night, the Imperial Guards began to cross the river in collapsible motorboats, which they had hauled through the jungle, and sampans taken from flooded rice fields. The bitterest battle of Malaya was about to begin. They landed and established a roadblock. Next morning in broad daylight more motorboats and sampans started crossing the river, and many were sunk by the Australian twenty-five pounders.

At first the Japanese were thrown back by the Australians but they still managed to land more troops on the riverbank. As the two Japanese divisions tried to force their way down the road, they made slow, bloody progress.

For forty-eight hours it was anybody's battle. Then the Australians and the Indians regained the initiative and began to push the Japanese back along the road.

At dawn on the third day a landing party of the Imperial Guards appeared in the British rear and cut them off. Japanese troops set up roadblocks so there would be no escape except into the swampy jungle on either side. This led to the most savage action of the whole campaign. As General Percival laconically reported: "The Japanese Guards fought with their traditional fanaticism." Even wounded Japanese, unable to walk and dying, crawled inch by inch out of the jungle, painfully pushing their rifles in front of them to take one more shot at the enemy.

The Australians and Indians retaliated with bitter ferocity, machine-gunning, bayoneting, and even clubbing the enemy with their rifles. All day, they charged the roadblocks. Brigadier Duncan, commander of the 45th Indian Brigade, was killed leading a bayonet charge, and Lieutenant Colonel Anderson, an Australian battalion commander, was awarded the Victoria Cross.

But bayonets and bravery cannot prevail against tanks and roadblocks. Realizing they could not fight their way out of Yamashita's trap, they decided to break up into small forces and make their way back to the British lines as best they could through the swampy jungle. By this time, most of the battalion commanders and other officers were dead. Out of a force of 4,500 men, only 450 Australians and 400 Indians rejoined the British main forces. They had abandoned all their guns and vehicles when they vanished into the jungle. The survivors, however, could feel proud—in a bloody, week-long battle, without tank or air support, they had held up Yamashita's whole army.

This battle had a curious effect on the arrogant General Nishimura and his elite troops. It was the first time they had come up against fierce, determined opposition, and whether this had anything to do with their subsequent behavior will always remain a matter of conjecture. After the battle, the Imperial Guards committed one of the worst atrocities in the Malayan campaign. They beheaded 200 wounded men that the Australians and Indians had left behind on the retreat into the jungle. The decapitation was observed by other British wounded hidden in the jungle, and after the war they gave evidence against the Guards at a war-crimes tribunal in Singapore.

Only a few days later, on another river crossing when British forces hastily retreated, the chaplain and the Royal Army Medical Corps orderlies bravely offered to stay behind and look after the wounded. The Japanese treated them quite well. General Percival reported: "Our men were not molested in any way by the Japanese on this occasion."

The Japanese themselves had been badly mauled in the Muar River battle. Among the seriously wounded was the commanding officer of Japan's most famous unit, the 3rd Regiment, which Yamashita had once commanded in Tokyo.

Nishimura felt that as commander of the Imperial Guards it was his prerogative to nominate the wounded colonel's successor. But Yamashita, who had grown impatient with Nishimura's uncooperative attitude, ignored him and signaled Headquarters at Saigon for a replacement of his own choice. This infuriated Nishimura and led to his waging a feud against Yamashita which nearly brought disaster to the Japanese Army in front of Singapore.

While he fought on the Muar River, Yamashita was preparing his left hook by moving his third division—the 18th—along the east coast as quickly as he could.

Just before the Muar River battle, Japanese troops wearing steel helmets, khaki shorts, and black jackets, like those worn forty years before in the Boxer Uprising, had been seen riding their bicycles near the swampy Endau River estuary, one hundred miles north of Johore Strait. On their first attempt to cross the shallow estuary, with its shoals and sandbanks, they were thrown back. This group had been an advance skirmishing force of the 18th Division.

Next day, an R.A.F. plane reported a big convoy sailing southward along the east coast of Malaya. Then it sighted two cruisers and twelve destroyers escorting two troopships and landing craft, which began to disembark troops near the Endau River.

The British realized that this was Yamashita's main attack, and sent two destroyers to intercept the Japanese transports. They engaged three Japanese destroyers and damaged one, but one British destroyer was sunk.

The last big air battle of the Malayan campaign also took place at this time. Every plane, including fifty Hurricanes that had just arrived from Britain, was flung into the fight. Obsolete Buffalo fighters escorted Hudsons, Wildebeests, and naval Albacore planes into the battle to try to sink the Japanese transports before the troops could land.

But Japanese Zero fighters, based on captured airfields in the north, swarmed up to meet them. These planes, which a year earlier Yamashita had judged better than the German Messerschmitts, were to give the British their final shock. Having placed great faith in the Hurricane reinforcements from England, they discovered that the Japanese Zeros were better, faster planes which shot the Hurricanes out of the sky. Although, according to the R.A.F., thirteen Zeros were destroyed, the British attack was driven off and the Japanese landed their troops. Even more disastrous for the British, the R.A.F. lost so many planes in this engagement that it was destroyed as a striking force in Malaya.

After this, the Japanese pushed rapidly ahead. The retreating Australians prepared an elaborate ambush on a rubber estate. The Japanese walked straight into it and in a fierce battle they lost 300 men. The Australian casualties were one hundred killed or missing.

This was the last fight on the Malayan mainland. That day, General Wavell in Java sent a signal to the British High Command, giving them discretion to withdraw from Malaya to Singapore Island. On the last night in January most of the remaining British troops crossed into Singapore.

At eight-fifteen the next morning, the Argyll and Sutherland Highlanders, who had formed the rear guard, marched, with their pipes skirling, across the Johore Causeway. Shortly afterward, there was a big explosion and a seventy-five foot gap was blown in the Causeway.

The siege of Singapore had begun.

CHAPTER 6

The White Man's Fortress

Seven hours after the Highlanders crossed the causeway, the Hirada Detached Troop—the vanguard of Yamashita's 5th Division—arrived at the rubber plantations on the banks of the Johore Strait.

That afternoon Yamashita had received a report that his patrols had cleared away enemy stragglers and reached the Strait. An hour later, he learned that the Imperial Guards had also arrived. Yamashita wrote in his diary:

The Imperial Guards and the 5th Division continue to advance, pressing hard on all fronts. At 16:47, the troops of the 5th Division advanced to the Johore Strait and are clearing the enemy remnants there. I am now preparing for my plan for Singapore, which I will attack within a week.

The next day he sent this report to Tokyo:

We have made an advance of 700 miles. This is the situation up to now: We have captured 330 guns, 400 heavy machine guns, 4,000 rifles, 280 armored cars and other vehicles, and repaired 250 bridges. We have taken 8,000 prisoners and estimate the enemy have 5,000 dead.

He moved his headquarters into a European bungalow on a rubber plantation just north of Johore and for four days worked on details of his attack on Singapore. The 5th and 18th Divisions were to lead the assault across the narrowest part of the Strait, followed by the Imperial Guards. He wanted to keep the Guards in reserve because he feared heavy fighting would take place not only when they tried to cross the Strait but also when they had a foothold on the island.

General Nishimura refused to believe that his Imperial Guards had not been chosen to lead the attack on the British fortress of Singapore, and he made a violent protest at Yamashita's conference with the divisional commanders. For Nishimura it was the last straw. He was still indignant over the replacement of the commander of the 3rd Regiment. Yamashita's own nominee from Saigon now commanded the famous 3rd.

When they drank sake in a toast to victory, Yamashita noticed that Nishimura hardly touched his and looked exceedingly sulky. Another general who only sipped from the small sake cup was Mutaguchi, who had arrived just a month before from Indochina to command the 18th Division in its landings on the Endau River and the assault on Singapore. He was famous in Japanese army circles as a drinking man. But he had sworn that his next drink would be only in Singapore.

Yamashita smiled at Mutaguchi's vow but not at the attitude of General Nishimura, who had now made it a matter of "face." When this situation happens in the East, it is always very difficult for the parties concerned to retract. They often get themselves into inextricable positions.

Yamashita's diary entry for February 6 said:

I handed over my orders at 11 A.M. to all the divisional commanders for the attack on Singapore. The commanders of the 18th and 5th Divisions said they would do their duty, but the divisional commander of the Imperial Guards looked very annoyed. He obviously has no faith in the plan. This plainly follows the demand he made yesterday that his division should lead the attack so he and his troops would be allowed to show their bravery.

Yamashita had no intention of changing his plan for any divisional commander, no matter how noble and distinguished. But he was worried—and within a day or two this was to be borne out by the facts—that Nishimura's attitude might have adverse effect on the attack on Singapore.

After the conference was over, Yamashita had a long talk with Lieutenant General Sosaku Suzuki, his chief of staff, who was a friend of Nishimura's. He asked him to go to the Imperial Guards and see if he could do anything to smooth things out. Suzuki found the Guards noncommittal and uncooperative. Nishimura and General Imaye entertained him civilly but refused to discuss the matter. When pressed by Yamashita's right-hand man, they simply said they had no opinion about the plan of battle.

While the Japanese generals were squabbling like this less than a mile away across the Strait, the British were preparing to defend their fortress. In the anticipation of a three-month siege, ammunition for each gun was limited to twenty rounds per day.

The British did not know that, because of the poor Japanese supply system, Yamashita was even shorter of ammunition. He had only a hundred rounds of small-arms ammunition for each soldier. In a long battle he was almost certain to be defeated, for the Japanese food rations were also in short supply—even his two-bowls-of-rice-a-day troops would be reduced to a near-starvation level.

What was the position in British-held Singapore? The Chief of the Imperial General Staff in London reported to the government that there were 100,000 men in Singapore, including 33,000 British troops and 17,000 Australians. He added: "It is doubtful that the Japanese have as many in the whole Malay Peninsula." The C.I.G.S. was correct. Yamashita, who had suffered over 5,000 casualties, had 30,000 men and 18 tanks left to attack Singapore and take its great naval base, valued at sixty-three million pounds sterling.

Singapore had been reinforced by the British 18th Division just before the Argylls marched over the Causeway. Two thousand Australian reinforcements had arrived the week before, but they were not the best troops, according to Gen-

eral Percival, who later had this to say about them in his
book *The War in Malaya:*

> Many Australians had only been in the army for a few
> weeks. They were excellent material but not soldiers yet.
> I have no wish to blame the authorities either in India
> or Australia for sending these untrained men. After all
> they had no better to send at the time. But I make these
> factual statements so that the problem may be under-
> stood. It was in fact one of the fruits of our failure to
> prepare for war. Let it not be forgotten also that these
> untrained men were included in all estimates of the
> garrison of Singapore Island.

Whether the reasons submitted by Percival were valid
or not, the Australian troops in Singapore were to write
the most inglorious chapter in the whole history of their
army.

In the first week in February, the Johore Strait was the
scene of strange isolated night patrols. Each side, afraid to
give its game away by employing boats, had troops swim
across to spy on the enemy. Japan and Australia are both
nations of strong swimmers, and the soldiers were easily
able to swim the thousand yards of the Strait. There were
also artillery duels, but they were fairly spasmodic, as each
side, unknown to the other, was trying to husband its ammunition.

A week after the British retreated to Singapore Island,
two Australian patrols who had been on the mainland twenty-
four hours swam back across the Strait just before dawn.
Their report was quickly taken to General Percival. Both
patrols said that very large Japanese forces, hiding in the
rubber plantations within a short distance of the Strait,
seemed to be preparing to move.

No sooner had they reported this than the first shells
began to drop on the 22nd Australian Brigade, part of the
Australian division which was holding the western end of
the Johore Strait. The Japanese Air Force began heavy
bombing of the naval base, the docks, and the airports.

In General Percival's view, "It was obvious that the
Japanese had brought up a lot more guns and had plenty
of ammunition." This was exactly what Yamashita wanted

him to think. He was in fact gambling most of his available ammunition on this great bluff.

The bombardment had begun at 10 A.M. and it continued to increase until after dark. The British described it as being "as great as on the western front in World War I." It was not, but then it was directed against a very small target.

During that day, against the wishes of his staff, Yamashita moved his battle headquarters into the Sultan's palace on the top of a hill in Johore, overlooking the Strait. It was only a mile away from the Australians and well within the range of small-arms and artillery fire. When his adjutant protested, he replied: "The enemy won't fire on this place. They would never dream I would come so near in such a prominent position."

He jotted down in his diary on February 8: "I command my army from Johore Palace, where I can look down on the coming field of battle."

And what a field of battle it was! The British had set fire to the Singapore oil tanks and flashes of gunfire illuminated the heavy black smoke from the burning oil. As darkness fell, the sky was lit up in a continuous flame as, fearing the attack was imminent, the British began to fire their biggest guns.

A Japanese swimming patrol reported after dark that they feared the British had fired the oil tanks so as to direct the blazing fuel into the Strait and set fire to the Japanese invasion forces. Yamashita received this report in silence. It was the obvious thing for them to do. Why it was not done is one of the many mysteries of the defense of Singapore.

On the night before the attack, Yamashita had an even graver concern. The Japanese were so short of food and ammunition that Colonel Ikatini, in charge of supplies, came to him and pleaded that he call it off. He warned that if the siege was prolonged it would probably fail through lack of ammunition and gasoline.

Yamashita refused to listen. He knew that if the British were allowed to hang on, they might obtain heavy reinforcements by sea and burst out of Singapore, then chase him up Malaya. He had to keep up the pressure until they broke, for the Japanese would have very little left if they lost the initiative. Yamashita was fully aware that, owing to the inefficiency of the Japanese Army rear organization, further supplies would take many weeks to arrive. While he was waiting for them, the British might discover his weakness in men as well as in materiel and attack him.

Later the Japanese general was to describe the situation like this:

My attack on Singapore was a bluff—a bluff that worked. I had 30,000 men and was outnumbered more than three to one. I knew that if I had to fight long for Singapore, I would be beaten. That is why the surrender had to be at once. I was very frightened all the time that the British would discover our numerical weakness and lack of supplies and force me into disastrous street fighting.

This was his position when he ordered the 5th Division to start the attack on Singapore. It was just before midnight when he went down to the Strait to watch the first troops cross in the landing barges he had brought down from Singora. He anticipated a bitter battle, lasting for days before he obtained a foothold on Singapore Island. However, half an hour after the Japanese barges loomed up in front of the Australians, the troops were ashore in large numbers.

No sooner had the Australians reported that armored landing craft and sampans had appeared in front of their positions than their telephone was cut. A few minutes later the Japanese were ashore at several points, and just after midnight they drove a wedge between the two Australian battalions defending the Strait.

As the Australians retreated, a red star shell was fired across the Strait, announcing that the 5th Division was safely ashore. Shortly afterward, a white star shell soared into the sky. This meant that the forward units of the 18th Division had also crossed the Strait. Just before dawn, Yamashita was so convinced that the battle was already won that he went to bed.

Half an hour after the first Japanese troops sailed across the Johore Strait, there was no doubt as to the result of the battle. In his book *The Fall of Singapore*, Frank Owen writes this tribute:

In about an hour the Japanese main invasion force established themselves firmly ashore. From this time onward they were bringing over from the Malayan mainland almost without interruption as many reinforcements and artillery, ammunition, tanks and transport as their barges would ferry. This remarkable achievement goes to the credit of the Japanese High Command in Malaya, especially the 18th and 5th divisions who made the initial landings.

Why did the Japanese gain a foothold so quickly? General Percival offers this explanation in his book *The War in Malaya*:

I believe it was solely due to the weakness of our defences which resulted from extended fronts. This was aggravated by the fact that again for reasons unknown our artillery defensive fire was slow in coming down.

That may have been due to the cutting of the telephone wires by the bombardment or to the fact that it is not easy to see signal lights in that wooded country.

On the other hand it seems there was an unfortunate reluctance to use the wireless. It also appears that the beach searchlights were never exposed. Some of them may have been destroyed by the bombardment. The chief reason why the Japanese got ashore was because we were too thin on the ground.

However tactfully and mildly the General put it, seldom has any commander indicted the incompetence, panic, and low morale of his own troops so strongly. This, allied to the cowardice and confusion among the Australians in the front line that night, gave General Yamashita the opportunity which more than justified his bluff.

Percival tried to excuse the conduct of his troops when he wrote:

Tactical movements at night in thick country in the middle of a battle which at many places was being fought at close quarters were undoubtedly too difficult. The result was much confusion and disorganization with groups of men becoming detached and lost.

These are conditions which produce stragglers and that there were stragglers in this case cannot be denied. These men were not long-service soldiers and discipline was not deep. The 22nd Australian Brigade fought against heavy odds in this battle. That may surprise some people who have received reports of an almost unopposed landing by a handful of Japanese.

Percival himself must take a great deal of the blame for the defeat. His assessment of the situation was as faulty as the behavior of so many of his troops. He said that the Japanese landed 13,000 troops that night and another 10,000 shortly before dawn. Actually, they landed less than half that number. But obviously the British commander had decided that he was being opposed by vastly superior forces. His estimation of Yamashita's resources was also tragically incorrect. This is borne out by a passage in his report: "In addition to the two attacking divisions there were two more divisions and probably three in reserve in Johore. This means that the Japanese had five or probably six divisions available for their attack on Singapore."

Since Percival based his estimate on the full Japanese divisional strength of 20,000 men, he assumed Yamashita had roughly 100,000 troops. Yet even if this had been true, the forces would only have been equal; instead, the British had more than three soldiers in Singapore for every Japanese in the whole of Malaya.

If Percival had had any inkling of the comparatively tiny army opposing him with its handful of tanks, a force dangerously short of food and ammunition, he might have done the one thing that Yamashita dreaded—put in a heavy counterattack and driven a wedge between the Japanese divisions. But Yamashita was not dealing with that sort of general. The man who, more than four years before, had so correctly forecast what the Japanese would do, was quite unable to cope with them in the field when they actually did it. He was a brilliant blueprint general, not a thrusting, hell-or-bust fighter like his enemy.

In spite of the unexpected success of his first landing, Yamashita was having more problems with the Imperial Guards. They were ordered to cross, the next day, into the swampy country at the mouth of the Kranji River, on Singapore Island. However, Nishimura, receiving a report of blazing oil seeping down into the water, still hesitated. He thought that the British had at last set the Strait afire. Making no attempt to verify the report—apparently given him by a single member of the swim patrol—he held up his division's attack without informing Yamashita.

If the Japanese had been faced with a more resolute enemy, Nishimura's disobedience might easily have led to the defeat of the invaders. A heavy counterattack, when Yamashita was short one division because Nishimura was hesitating on the wrong bank of the Strait, might have caused his other troops to be thrown back into the water.

Yamashita spent most of the first day of the battle watching the fighting from the bank of the Strait. Singapore was now a mass of flames and many buildings across the water could be seen burning fiercely.

Just over twenty-four hours after his first forward troops landed on Singapore Island, he moved his headquarters across the Strait, traveling just before dawn with his staff officers in a landing barge which was so crowded that they all had to stand upright with their hands on one another's shoulders to keep from falling overboard. In fact, his deputy chief of staff, Major General Manaki, did fall from the barge and was nearly drowned in the darkness before he was fished out again.

When Yamashita and his party set foot in Singapore, it was still dark and they could not see anything clearly. Colonel Tsuji, the planning officer, who was stumbling up the bank, trod on something soft and a loud shriek resounded in the darkness near his feet. Shining a carefully shaded flashlight, he discovered groups of British prisoners lying on the ground, tied together with ropes.

Shortly after Yamashita set up headquarters on Singapore Island, he received the news that the Imperial Guards were still on the mainland of Malaya. This is how he recorded it in his diary:

> I ordered the Imperial Guards who were waiting among the rubber plantations to cross the Strait. I wanted them to go in after the 5th Division's crossing, but then their commander asked for further orders from me. I received a message from him that his troops were hesitating to cross because of oil flames on the surface of the water. It looks to me as if he is still upset about not being able to lead the attack. I ordered him to do his duty.

Following a peremptory order from the Army commander, Nishimura's division immediately began to sail up the Kranji

River and wade ashore in the mangrove swamps. The tide was rising now, and many of his troops were drowned as they tried to struggle ashore, waist-deep in the mud. In addition, the burning oil, which was now flowing more rapidly from the blazing tanks, had seeped into the mud and many of the Guards were burned alive. Several more were killed by heavy machine-gun and mortar fire from the 27th Australian Brigade, which was defending the Kranji Peninsula. Nevertheless, by midday the Guards had fought their way ashore and were established in force on Singapore Island. But by his hesitation, Nishimura had lost many more men than he need have.

Meanwhile, hundreds of other Japanese troops were working to repair the blown-up Johore Causeway. Again the British had bungled, and the gap in the Causeway was much more easily repaired than it should have been. Japanese foot soldiers were crossing it within a day of the first landings, and a few hours later, Japanese vehicles were being driven onto the island. In addition, Yamashita managed to float over in his barges half a dozen tanks, which went into action immediately. By the afternoon, the Japanese forces were on the edge of Tengah airfield and British troops were firing forty-centimeter fortress guns point-blank at them.

Singapore was rapidly becoming a nightmare. The burning black smoke from the blazing oil made both soldiers and civilians look like miners. Confusion, panic, and depression were rife among the garrison.

General Wavell came from Java to consult with General Percival and the Australian Expeditionary Force commander, General Gordon Bennett. The meeting took place at General Bennett's headquarters in some estate buildings near the road junction at Bukit Timah, on a hill overlooking Singapore. The Japanese shelling was now so heavy that the three generals had to continue their conference crouching under a table to escape the shellfire. One shell exploded so near that it blew up Percival's car outside and a splinter smashed his glasses.

General Wavell flew back to Java with depressing reports from the front. The 44th Indian Brigade, for instance, suddenly retreated four miles. One battalion had been given permission to withdraw, because of heavy bombing and machine-gunning from the air, and when the rest of the brigade saw this, they panicked and went back with them. Percival again ruefully reported: "It was the fault of raw troops with inexperienced commanders."

Yamashita's tanks were now in action and although anti-tank guns held them off for a short time, they gradually forced the British troops back. Hastily, a counterattack was planned, but once again the decision was taken too late. The Japanese attacked first and came down Bukit Timah Road while the British troops were still forming.

February 11 was Japan's National Day, on which Yamashita had hoped to make a triumphal entry into Singapore. But his schedule had been held up by the fierce battle at the Muar River, so instead, on that day he ordered the Japanese to scatter surrender leaflets over Singapore. They threw out twenty envelopes addressed to "Excellency British Commander," calling upon him to surrender.

Yamashita was becoming very concerned. After the first landing, his attack had not moved quite as swiftly as he had hoped although he had employed his full forces. Now he was running dangerously short of ammunition—particularly rifle bullets—and must effect the surrender of Singapore before his ammunition ran out altogether. Otherwise, there was an even chance he would be defeated.

The end, however, was very near. The Singapore naval base had been blown up and additional clouds of black smoke were eddying over the battleground. More smoke came from the big Indian base hospital, which was burning down. Yamashita moved his headquarters to a wrecked factory near Bukit Timah and issued his orders for the last all-out assault.

The British seemed to be trying to shorten their line and preparing to dig in until reinforcements reached them. This was Yamashita's greatest fear. He kept sending urgent signals to the Japanese Navy and Air Force to keep constant watch for any sea-borne reinforcements nearing the beleaguered city. He would have been even less happy if he had known that he had underestimated the strength of his enemy. He thought there were 40,000 troops in Singapore; there were more than twice as many.

His final plan was to ring the city as nearly as he could and use the Imperial Guards, which he had held in semi-reserve, for the final assault. General Nishimura, however, true to the attitude he had maintained throughout the campaign, did not obey the order to move up for the final battle. As soon as Yamashita heard this, he dispatched Colonel

Tsuji to the Imperial Guards to ask what had happened now. It was a most serious situation because his other two divisions, who had borne the brunt of the fighting, were tired and had suffered many casualties.

First of all, Nishimura said that he could not understand the order. When Colonel Tsuji began to cross-examine them about it, both the divisional commander and his chief of staff, Major General Imaye, said angrily that they were not prepared to discuss the matter with an officer of lower rank.

In this tense situation, the threat of a counterattack at any moment and the fate of Singapore trembling in the balance, Yamashita had to send his deputy chief of staff, Major General Manaki, to Imperial Guards Headquarters with a written order for them to move into position. Only then did they start to move toward their position near the reservoir.

On the British side, too, a general was behaving strangely. Gordon Bennett, upset because his Australians had let the Japanese land on Singapore after only twenty-five minutes of fighting, was rapidly losing heart for the fight. He sent off a secret message to the Australian Prime Minister, saying that if any other formations fell back, he intended to surrender to save needless loss of life. He omitted to tell his commanding officer, General Percival, that he had sent this message. He also managed to escape from Singapore while General Percival and the other senior British officers surrendered.

In contrast to this behavior, many soldiers fought with desperate bravery. The Malay Regiment, fighting for their homeland, held up the Japanese for two days and nearly all of them died at their posts. And when the Imperial Guards eventually went into action, they were thrown back by the 2nd Indian Brigade.

But Singapore itself was rapidly becoming a shambles. All the shops and offices were deserted and damaged by shellfire and bombing. Mutilated corpses lay unburied, blackening and stinking in the hot streets. Water seeped from drains smashed by shells. The blackened, grimy, sweaty troops fought on, although each hour brought more depressing rumors and frightening facts. Explosion after explosion, more places were demolished, and the troops realized that the battle was nearly over. It was estimated that the water supply would not last more than another forty-eight hours.

There were a million people in the city, many of them

refugees from the mainland of Malaya. Frantic, screaming Indians continued to roam the streets in their futile search for safety. But the Chinese, who made up most of the population, were nowhere to be seen. They remained indoors, waiting for the end.

General Percival sent a telegram to General Wavell in Java, urging that he be given the "widest discretionary powers"—in other words, surrender. At first, the answer was no, but after several more signals, Wavell reluctantly gave him permission to do what he thought was best.

Another dreadful incident occurred at this time. Yamashita's troops, now in great force on the outskirts of Singapore, got out of hand in the excitement of battle and committed more atrocities. General Percival gave the following account in his book:

> The Japanese troops entered the great military hospital at Alexandra and there a tragedy took place. They claimed that Indian troops had fired from the hospital. Whether they did so or not, I cannot say.
>
> As a reprisal they bayoneted some members of the staff and patients including one poor fellow as he lay on the operating table. Next day they murdered 150 of the staff and patients. There were many horrors in the last war but for cold-blooded barbarity this deed will surely rank very high.

It was the worst massacre since the Imperial Guards had gone berserk and murdered two hundred British wounded on the banks of the Muar River. This atrocity, equally upsetting to both commanders, was the type of behavior which Yamashita dreaded increasingly as his troops became drunk with easy victory. Throughout the campaign, he kept sending notes to, and conferring with, his political officers about "the education of our troops."

General Percival, though not the most brilliant or audacious general, was a very fair-minded man. He wrote: "I did what I could at the surrender to ensure the safety of both troops and civilians. In this connection it should be recorded that General Yamashita never allowed the main body of his troops to enter Singapore City."

There were many other things on Percival's mind before the surrender. Not only water was running short but also artillery ammunition and gasoline—because millions of gallons had been destroyed. Percival held an urgent last conference with the Governor, Sir Shenton Thomas, in the Singapore Club. In surroundings reminiscent of their past glory, an air of pompous unreality still clung closely to them. The British General, wearing his coal-scuttle helmet and wide-khaki shorts, still had a polished Sam Browne belt, and the Governor wore his starched but crumpled white suit.

The slowness with which they reacted to the situation throughout is typified by a memorandum which the Governor had sent to the Malayan Civil Service as Yamashita approached Singapore. It said: "The day of minute papers has gone. There must be no more passing of files from one department to another. In the great majority of cases a decision can be taken or obtained after a brief conversation by telephone or direct. The essential thing is speed in action." The *Straits Times* sourly observed that this announcement had come at least two years too late.

And General Percival wrote this on Saturday, February 14: "At Fort Canning we have taken over one of the adjoining houses and an improvised mess has been established here. The Chinese servants as usual rose to the occasion and ran a wonderful show considering their difficulties and the numbers they had to cater for."

Next day, he surrendered Singapore.

The first indication of the surrender occurred at one o'clock. Captain Sugita, of the foremost company of the Japanese 5th Division a mile away from Bukit Timah, saw three British officers standing up and waving a white flag. The British —Major General Newbiggin, Captain Wild, and the secretary to the Governor of Malaya—walked across the lines toward him while his troops held their fire.

Sugita at once signaled Headquarters for Yamashita's orders. The General's message said: "We accept their surrender. The Japanese commander will meet them at 1800 hours."

Yamashita noted in his diary: "When the message came of the enemy surrender offer, I was very cautious about it. I was afraid it might be a trick. I ordered the British commander with his chief of staff and interpreter to meet me at 1800 hours. I also ordered a guard of one thousand armed soldiers to protect us at the meeting place."

The trick he feared was a ruse to stall off fighting until

supplies and reinforcements arrived, so he sent a simultaneous signal to the Japanese Air Force: "Keep a sharp lookout for any enemy reinforcements and sink them."

The two generals met at the Ford factory at Bukit Timah, which had been heavily shelled and was half ruined. Percival did not arrive until half an hour after the appointed time, and it was nearly seven o'clock in the evening before the two commanders met face to face.

They sat opposite each other at a long table covered with a white cloth, each general surrounded by four or five staff officers. The room was rather dark, but Yamashita could see that Percival was very pale and his hands were shaking. Every window, every opening in the bomb-shattered walls, was crowded with cameramen and reporters. After the introduction was made by the Japanese interpreter, they shook hands formally. This is Yamashita's account of the meeting:

On this occasion I was supposed to have spoken to Percival rather abruptly. If I did, it was because I now realized that the British army had about 100,000 men against my three divisions of 30,000 men. They also had many more bullets and other munitions than I had.

There have been many versions and rumors about my behavior at this meeting, including the story that I said to him, "All or nothing." This is not true. But I knew that if the battle was to be fought in the streets of Singapore, there would be many casualties among the civilian population, and I did not know how long we could carry on, as our munitions were very low. I was preparing an all-out attack on that night and their surrender offer came as a surprise.

After making a promise to meet me, the enemy commander was half an hour late; when the time came to talk, he accepted the unconditional surrender but asked me to postpone the cease-fire until the next day.

It looked to me as if the British Army wanted to delay everything but they still estimated the Japanese forces as more than they really were. They seemed to assess our force at about five divisions.

I was afraid in my heart that they would discover that our forces were much less than theirs. That was why I decided that I must use all means to make them surrender without terms. My interpreter was very poor.

Obviously, he did not know about my worries and he also had difficulty with technical army terms. I became irritated, as I wanted to bring the matter straight to a conclusion, and I told my interpreter, "I want to hear nothing from him except yes or no."

I am afraid that in my anxiety I emphasized the "yes or no" in English too much. The interpreter also emphasized the words very loudly when he repeated them to the British commander. This, however, did end the matter quickly and Percival agreed to my demand for unconditional surrender.

The reporters who heard my words "yes or no" thought I was being haughty. I have no excuse for that but I have been annoyed ever since by the newspapers reporting with such glee how I spoke so harshly and with such fierceness. I have never tried to make any excuse for it publicly but I would like people to know my real state of mind on that occasion.

In the diary written by his adjutant, the incident is discussed as follows.

The meeting between the two army commanders ended at 1900 when the enemy accepted unconditional surrender. Yamashita stood up and again shook hands with the enemy commander. He was surrounded by heaps of cameramen and war reporters. He told me afterward that he wanted to say a few kind words to Percival while he was shaking hands with him, as he looked so pale and thin and ill. But he could not say anything because he does not speak English, and he realized how difficult it is to convey heartfelt sympathy when the words are being interpreted by a third person.

After the surrender, Yamashita went to bed at eleven o'clock, but he could not sleep. Several times he got up and walked about.

Just before dawn, his chief of staff, Lieutenant General Suzuki, heard him walk out of the door. Singapore was quiet at last. There was no gunfire but there was a strong smell of cordite, and smoke drifted from the city. It was still dark and there were milky clouds in the sky.

Suzuki, worried that his commander in chief was wandering about in the dark without an escort, quietly followed him. As dawn broke, he watched him standing at the edge of the wood. He slowly faced the direction of the Emperor's Palace in Tokyo and began praying and bowing ceremoniously.

It was Yamashita's finest hour. He had conquered, on behalf of the Japanese Emperor, Britain's greatest bastion. He had also destroyed the white man's sovereignty in the East forever. Whether he realized it or not, no one can tell. But the world was never to be the same after what this Japanese general accomplished that night.

The next day, Captain Sugita, the man who had reported the British white flag of surrender, headed a victory march through the nearly deserted streets and smoking ruins of the captured city. He hoisted the triumphant Rising Sun flag of Nippon over the British Governor's residence. The Emperor sent an imperial envoy with a message wrapped in scarlet silk on which was written, in an ancient Japanese script which only the Son of Heaven can use, "I praise thee all."

Meanwhile, Yamashita plunged into the tangled administrative details of moving into captivity 100,000 prisoners of war. In the middle of all the rejoicing, he made this note: "Some of our men don't know how to treat British officers, and their behavior seems impolite to me. I have given instructions that they must be more polite to surrendered officers." As all the world knows, few Japanese took notice of these orders.

Nishimura, the Imperial Guards commander, retained his uncooperative attitude even in the hour of victory. When he heard that Yamashita had arranged a memorial service for the dead of his 25th Army, he held one for his own division the day before, without inviting his commander in chief. It was the last straw. Although he still remained outwardly polite, Yamashita reported the whole matter to his superior, Count Terauchi, commander of the Southern Region. As a result of their leader's behavior in the campaign, the Imperial Guards did not receive the Emperor's citation for the capture of Singapore, which was received by the other two divisions. This was considered the supreme disgrace for the Guards.

Shortly after the fall of Singapore, Nishimura was relieved of his command and retired to Japan, where he took no further part in the war. After the Japanese surrender, he was brought back to Singapore, tried and convicted as a war criminal, and hanged for the massacre on the Muar River.

Nishimura's second in command, Major General Imaye, was demoted and made a regimental commander in Manchuria. During the Russian invasion in the last few days of the war, he was captured; he died in a Siberian prison camp.

Seventy days after the first troops of the Japanese 5th Division had waded ashore in the little port of Singora in Thailand, seven hundred miles to the north, Britain's greatest fortress had fallen. General Percival, the defeated commander, summed up the British view of the campaign as follows in his book:

Singapore was the place above all the Japanese wanted to capture and against it they threw the pick of their armed forces. Of what did these forces consist? I have seen it stated that a 100,000 British surrendered to 30,000 Japanese. That, of course, is sheer nonsense.

Does anyone seriously think the Japanese would be so foolish as to try to win the prize they wanted so badly with 30,000 men? It is safer to say they employed 150,000 men in Malaya, although some Japanese reports suggest a much higher figure. They also employed two tank regiments probably containing 200–300 tanks.

For their attack on Singapore the Japanese employed 68,000 combat troops in addition to other units. There can be little doubt that at the end of the campaign there were over 100,000 Japanese troops on Singapore Island and in south Malaya. They had fresh troops in action every 36 hours while our troops were fighting for weeks on end without rest.

Percival then adds this remark: "The Japanese are a secretive race and it is never easy to get accurate information on military subjects." There is no doubt that although he vastly exaggerated the size of the enemy that overcame him General Percival wrote this in good faith. These estimates clearly reveal his attitude toward an enemy whom he obviously regarded as numerically overwhelming and unbeatable.

His report on the Japanese Air Force was a little more nearly accurate. He wrote that the Japanese 3rd Air Division had 670 aircraft, including 100 heavy bombers, and that 270 replacement aircraft were later flown from Japan, giving a total of 940. Actually, the total number of Japanese Army and Navy aircraft used in the campaign was 799.

Of the British resources General Percival wrote:

The total number of our officers and men was 125,000 although the strength in Malaya at any one time was considerably less than this. It also included administrative troops and unarmed troops owing to the shortage of personal weapons. There were 85,000 British troops in the Singapore area but they included poorly trained and administrative troops and we never had more than one squadron of light tanks.

Summing up the Malayan campaign, he said: "The Japanese total casualties will never perhaps be known accurately but undoubtedly they will be heavy."

They were not. Japanese casualties in the Malayan campaign were 3,507 dead and 6,150 wounded. Their casualties in the victorious battle for Singapore were: 1,715 dead, 3,378 wounded; total: 5,093. Just over 1,700 dead was a very small price to pay for the greatest victory that Asians had won against the white man since the wild Mongol horsemen of Genghis Khan stood at the gates of Vienna centuries before.

CHAPTER 7

On Guard Against the Russians

Yamashita became Japan's greatest war hero after the fall of Singapore, but he was never allowed to enjoy his triumph. Premier Tojo once again picked up on his sensitive political antennae whispers that many generals in Imperial Headquarters wanted Yamashita to be War Minister. The post, which could only be held by a military man, was technically vacant. When Tojo had been promoted to Premier, he still retained the War Ministry. By not appointing a successor for the job, he felt he was insuring himself against any powerful rival.

The man who had pressed the button for the bombing of Pearl Harbor moved with his usual ruthless swiftness when he heard the whispers. Yamashita was in Singapore, drafting the victory report which he was to read before the Emperor, when he recevied a signal posting him back to Manchuria.

His transfer was effected with such secrecy that only a few senior officers knew about it. He was even refused permission to have a short leave in Tokyo on his way to Manchuria. Tojo was determined that Yamashita should not report to the Emperor in person—prerogative of any successful Japanese general—because he felt this might clinch the War Ministry job.

The premier's sudden transfer of his most successful general was a stroke of political genius. Although heavily embroiled with Britain and America, the Japanese never took their eyes off the Russian frontier. Russia had been their traditional enemy for nearly forty years, ever since they had beaten her in the Russo-Japanese War. They were afraid now that the Soviet Union was just biding her time to inflict a crushing blow upon Japan and avenge her defeat.

Throughout the most disastrous part of the war, the Japanese seldom had less than 500,000 troops standing on the Russian frontier in Manchuria. This force was divided into two parts, of which the most important was the 1st Army Group, based in Botanko, on the Siberian border. In the event of war, its task was to cut across the peninsula and isolate Vladivostok, Russia's most easterly port, only six hundred miles from Japan. This was a vital part of Japanese strategy. If they took Vladivostok, they would have a major port from which to reinforce their armies in Manchuria. In addition, the Russians themselves would be prevented from using it as a base against Japan.

On the left flank was the 2nd Army Group. In the event of war, it would swing northward its first objective being the cutting off of the Trans-Siberian railway.

Yamashita was assigned to lead the 1st Army Group. If war came with Russian, it would be the most important field command in the Japanese Army. Tojo, therefore, could always reassure anybody—including the Emperor—that Japan's best general was standing in a key position on the Siberian frontier, ready to deal with the Russians if they attacked. Meanwhile, the premier's biggest rival would be a long way from Tokyo during most of the war.

Yamashita concealed his disappointment at Tojo's refusal to allow him to visit his homeland on the way to Botanko. The nearest he got to Japan was Formosa, where the local headquarters tried to cheer him up, Japanese style, by sending three of the most beautiful geisha they could find to call on him. Yamashita, who never shared the ordinary Japanese appetite for casual women, told his adjutant: "I know they want to please me with these girls, but send them back—and don't forget to tip them." He then took supper alone in his room.

His adjutant noted: "When General Yamashita received his orders to go to Manchuria, I know he tried several times to negotiate with Imperial Headquarters to allow him to stop at Tokyo, but they refused. He never discussed it, but I knew

This photograph, one of the few showing Yamashita in civilian clothes, was taken when he was a lieutenant. It was his favorite photograph, and he often gave it to friends signed with a cordial message.

Captain Yamashita and his bride, Hisako Nagayama.

Yamashita meets Mussolini in the Palazzo Venezia, Rome, in May, 1941, and reads a message of greeting from Premier Tojo. On Mussolini's left is his Army chief, General Cavallero, and behind him is General Pricolo, Commander of the Italian Air Force. Standing by Yamashita is his interpreter, Colonel Shimizu. Behind him are (left to right) Major Generals Hara and Ayabe.

The fateful meeting between Hitler and Yamashita in the Berlin Chancellery, January, 1941, before the Japanese undertook a five-month tour of German war factories and installations. At extreme right is Field Marshal Keitel, Chief of the German armed forces. Back to camera, seated on the sofa, is Hitler's personal adjutant, Colonel Schmundt. With Yamashita is Major General Okamoto.

From behind a camouflaged emplacement, Yamashita in 1942 watches Russian troop movements in Siberia, just over the Manchurian border.

Yamashita leading his staff down the trail to Item Company, September 2, 1945.

Colonel Barlow and other U. S. soldiers confront Yamashita and his staff soon after the Japanese had crossed U. S. lines to surrender.

General Jonathan Wainwright, seated at extreme left, and British Lieutenant General A. E. Percival, British commander at Singapore, seated fourth from left, attend the ceremony during which Yamashita surrenders all Japanese forces in the Philippines.

The gates of New Bilibid Prison close behind General Yamashita.

Yamashita on the witness stand during the War Crimes Trial.

he was very lonely and sad because he could not visit his homeland."

Wherever Yamashita went at this time, senior officers eyed him with interest; few doubted that his move to Manchuria was due solely to Tojo's jealousy and fear of him. Although they recognized that to be an army-group commander was every general's ambition, they felt a soldier of his caliber was being wasted in Manchuria in the middle of their country's greatest war.

Ironically enough, another general was traveling the same route at the same time, but in very different circumstances. A few months after the fall of Singapore, Yamashita's defeated opponent, General Percival, was taken on a Japanese transport to Formosa, on his way to a Manchurian prison camp.

Yamashita arrived at Botanko in such great secrecy that he was called "the General in a mask." One officer wrote: "General Yamashita did not take off his mask all the time he he was in the Manchurian Army. He was not allowed to step into Japan. There was a complete news censorship on his movements and no newspaper reported his transfer."

The security blackout was total. The ostensible reason was to avoid alarming the Russians with his presence. But the Soviet spy system was so efficient that there is little doubt they were fully aware the Tiger of Malaya had arrived on the Siberian frontier.

However, the secrecy continued to be enforced. Yamashita's first act when he arrived in Botanko was to give orders to enlarge the dining room of his requisitioned house, so that all his entertaining might be done at home. During the whole period he was in Manchuria, he never entered a restaurant, and he ordered his staff officers never to mention his name or talk about him in public places.

His wife, Hisako, soon joined him in this lonely, remote life. At first, he would not permit her to come, because he felt he should not have a privilege denied his troops. But when the wife of another general was due to come to Manchuria, he was finally persuaded to allow Mrs. Yamashita to travel with her.

The Yamashitas lived in a requisitioned house, sixty miles from the Russian frontier, with an antiaircraft gun and an air-raid shelter in the garden. The days and months went by quietly, almost boringly, with constant troop maneuvers, often lasting three days at a time, and long conferences afterward to discuss the training schemes. Most of Yamashita's time was spent trying to perfect the Japanese infantry in the close artillery-support schemes, used to attack concrete emplacements, which he had watched Hitler's troops perform in Germany just before the outbreak of war.

There was only one little piece of excitement. Six months after he arrived in Manchuria, Yamashita was holding a conference of divisional commanders when an orderly brought him a telegram. He glanced at it for a moment, turned toward the Imperial Palace in Tokyo, and saluted. Then, without a word, he walked out of the room. No one dared to ask him what the telegram contained, but four days later it was officially announced he had been promoted to full general. Being a good soldier, he had not told anyone until the announcement was official. His only comment was: "It is extremely difficult to be a lieutenant general, but to be any good as a full general is mostly a matter of luck." He celebrated his promotion with sweet bean cakes and sake in his enlarged dining room.

The war in Burma and the Pacific was a constant topic of conversation among Japanese officers in this Manchurian backwater. One day, when the officers in the mess were discussing the Pacific war, one of them said: "I suspect things are not going too well at the moment."

Yamashita interposed sharply: "It does not matter what happens in the Pacific. Our eyes and ears do not face south, toward the Pacific. Our duty is to face north, toward Russia."

Privately, however, he was not so indifferent to Japan's war fortunes. In July, 1944, the Americans captured the tiny Pacific island of Saipan, only 1,300 miles from the Japanese mainland. It was the first significant American victory of the war, and meant that Japan was now within range of land-based enemy bombers. Meanwhile, the Japanese march on India was flung back by the British on the Burma border. For the first time since their runaway victories in the Pacific and Asia, the Japanese faced the possibility not only of defeat but of the destruction of their homeland.

Yamashita, in faraway Manchuria, was fully aware of this situation. His first reaction was to have his wife ask her parents to leave Tokyo and stay in Kamakura, a seaside resort nearby, in case air raids began. He also began to talk to his wife about adopting his brother's son Kumiyo. Since they had no children, several times it had been suggested that they adopt one of his doctor brother's sons. It is very common in Japan for a man with several sons to allow a member of his family who is childless to adopt one. The child becomes the adopter's legal descendant, to carry on his name in that branch of the family. Yamashita had always refused abruptly to entertain the idea. Now, suddenly, he told his wife to write to Tokyo and find out if his brother would still be agreeable to the adoption.

Three days after the fall of Saipan, Yamashita received a telephone call from General Yoshigiro Umezu, commander of the Kwantung Armies, who was in Singking, the Headquarters of the Manchurian Army Group. Umezu asked him to fly and see him at once, and when he arrived, they had a long talk in a private room for many hours.

Umezu told him that, as a result of the American advance in the Pacific, Tojo was finished. He outlined the political situation in Tokyo, saying that the government was in confusion and despair and facing a serious crisis. A strong group wanted to continue the war, but insisted that before going on they make peace with Chiang Kai-shek in China while that was still possible.

Others wanted to send an envoy to Russia, and use the Kremlin as an intermediary to make a negotiated peace with the Allies. Umezu said he was very much against this proposal, for in his view, the Russians would immediately recognize it as a sign of weakness. Their only reply would probably be to invade Manchuria—which is exactly what they did at the end of the war.

Next day, Tojo fell. He had been Premier for nearly three years. A new Cabinet was formed by Kuniaki Koiso, and from then on, things began to move rapidly. The new Cabinet's main job was to prepare for the coming Allied invasion while at the same time keeping the Japanese, who were now a hungry, cold, and ragged nation, believing in a final victory.

The negotiations with Chiang Kai-shek came to nothing. In spite of Yamashita's advice, feelers were sent to Russia, but after weeks of maneuvering, the Soviet Union firmly rejected the Japanese peace emissary.

Six weeks after the fall of Saipan, Yamashita received a not unexpected signal ordering him to Tokyo at once. When he packed up his kit, several officers suggested that his wife should remain in Manchuria now that the war was going against them. But the old-fashioned Japanese general, who rarely said anything about domestic matters, told her abruptly: "It is your duty to suffer in the land of your ancestors. You will return to Japan at once."

Before he left for Tokyo, he gave his wife a parcel wrapped in oilskin. He told her she must carry it unopened to Kamakura and take great care of it. At the end of the war, she opened the package and found it contained the diaries he had written in Malaya and Singapore and all his maps. There were also other important papers, including a draft of the lecture, telling the story of his Singapore victory, which he had prepared to give in front of the Emperor, but which Tojo had prevented him from delivering. She buried this package in the garden, to prevent the Americans from taking it away.

Yamashita's departure at dawn from Singking Army Headquarters was unannounced, just as at Singapore, and he was seen off only by one or two of his personal staff. That evening, he stepped on Japanese soil for the first time in nearly three years. When he reported to Imperial Headquarters, he was told that he had been appointed to command the 14th Army Group, to defend the Philippines against the coming American invasion.

He found that the generals were not unanimous about his new appointment. There was a very strong opinion among many of them that Japan's best general should not be wasted in the Philippines. Appreciating that those islands must soon fall and that the battle would start moving rapidly toward Japan's own shores, they wanted Yamashita to remain and lead a last defense of the homeland.

But Marquis Koichi Kido, Lord Keeper of the Privy Seal, wanted him to take command in the Philippines, and this enigmatic official, one of the several mysterious figures flitting around the throne, had the Emperor's ear. Yamashita was posted to Manila.

Yamashita's personal reaction to the situation was to have further long talks with his wife on how soon the adoption of his brother's son could be pushed through. He urged her to rush the matter, as he would not have much time in Tokyo.

"When he went to Singapore," Mrs. Yamashita later recalled, "I felt nothing. This time I felt an ill omen. I felt I would never see him again. He obviously had the same feeling, otherwise he would not have been suddenly so anxious to adopt a son. He thought he was going to be killed in battle."

CHAPTER 8

The Battle He Did Not Want

The Japanese High Command continued to plan victory operations, which they named Sho. In the realization that the Americans would invade the Philippines as the next major steppingstone toward Japan, they gave the defense of these islands first priority, naming it Sho One. They had already drawn up their plans, estimating that ten divisions with five independent brigades would be sufficient to hold the Philippines.

However, not all was well in the Japanese-occupied Philippines. General Homma, the man who had chased MacArthur out of the Philippines in 1942, had been recalled to Tokyo shortly afterward. There is little doubt that, as the other victorious Japanese general who had received a great deal of publicity, he like Yamashita was a victim of Tojo's jealousy.

Homma's replacement, Lieutenant General Shijenori Kuroda, who had spent years training in England with the British Army, was a very peculiar person. For instance, he never had much faith that the Japanese would win the war. Before the Tojo Cabinet fell he told the chief of Army intelligence at Imperial Headquarters: "It would be best to sue for immediate peace before the Americans come and destroy our nation by air power." He also disapproved of the construction of Air Force bases at Tacloban and other places on Leyte Island, pointing out that because they were not to be used immediately, "It amounts to construction for the use of the enemy." The fact that only a few months later he was to be proved exactly right did nothing to endear him to the Japanese High Command.

For a long time, Imperial Headquarters had not been happy about Kuroda's stewardship in the Philippines, but as he was Tojo's nominee, there was little they could do about it. As soon as Tojo fell, they wasted no time. They flew a special personnel officer from Tokyo to investigate various stories which had been circulating about his behavior. These reports stated that he had been "devoting too much time to golf, reading, and personal matters." The personal matters, so discreetly mentioned, were the entertainment of geisha and other accommodating girls in his official residence every night. In addition, discipline had been allowed to become lax and Kuroda was on bad terms with many of his senior officers. Headquarters also recognized the fact that the Japanese occupation troops, most of whom had been in the Philippines for more than two years, had grown soft and had little will to fight. When the special investigating officer filed his report in Tokyo after three weeks in the islands, Kuroda was sacked at once. Yamashita was given his job.

Campaign-planning conferences started the day he arrived in Tokyo. From the start, he behaved in the slightly eccentric manner which was known but not always appreciated. While the Chief of War Plans was outlining the defense strategy, Yamashita closed his eyes and began snoring. The Chief said rather coldly: "Perhaps you are tired, General. Would you like to take a rest?"

Yamashita slowly opened his eyes and replied, "Please continue. I was just considering your plan. How many islands, for instance, are there in the Philippines?"

He was told there were four thousand. "How do you expect me to draw up a defense plan for four thousand islands?" Yamashita exclaimed. "The enemy can make an unexpected attack on several of them at once. I must have the guaranteed help of the Air Force and Navy to enable me to defend the territory."

His next question was unexpected: "How have you been treating the Catholic population there?" There was a great deal of consultation before he was told finally that the welfare of the Catholic population was left to the Army Commanders on the spot.

Possibly foreseeing the grave Filipino guerrilla problem which was to face him when he arrived, he said: "I do not agree that the Army on the spot should have been allowed to deal with the very large number of Catholics there. I think we should have been at great pains to give them leadership. If we have not done so, how can you expect these people to support us? When I get there, I will look into the matter but it can be a grave military problem."

Promising him their full support in all these matters, Imperial Headquarters issued these orders to Yamashita:

1. As leader of the 14th Army Group, under the command of Field Marshal Count Hisaichi Terauchi, C. in C. Southern Region, he must defend the whole Philippines. Fullest cooperation would be given to him by Naval Headquarters—a separate command at Manila led by Admiral Soemu Toyoda.
2. If the United States forces should attack, the Army would have the cooperation of the Navy and the Air Force. Army reinforcements would be sent for the defense of the Philippines.
3. He would cooperate with the Philippine government to keep the peace, but any negotiations with that government would be carried out only by the commander of the Southern Region and Imperial Headquarters.

Exactly a week after his arrival in his native country, Yamashita left Japan for the last time. He spent the night in Formosa—having dodged several American planes, which were already becoming very numerous in the Pacific—and arrived in Manila the next evening.

There he found that American air activity was increasing daily. A fortnight before his arrival, American bombers had staged their first big attack on the Manila naval base. Now they raided it several times a day, and the harbor was full of sunken ships. The town was blacked out at night and the air raids were so constant and heavy that no vehicles could move in the daytime.

Yamashita's first act was to call a meeting of officers at Fort McKinley, the former American base. He stood on a platform in the blacked-out hall and said: "I have been told by our Emperor that the crisis will develop first on this battle-field. This gives us all a heavy responsibility. I expect you to fight bravely, bearing in mind that victories are won only by resolute and united men. If we all remember this, the Jap-anese Army must win in the end."

He spoke for twenty minutes, and everyone in the hall was silent, but great exhilaration followed his speech. The fact that the conqueror of Singapore had taken over cheered up a demoralized army which had spent three years in the peaceful occupation of these tropical islands under an indif-ferent commander. No one had heard of Yamashita since the fall of Singapore—some even believed him to be dead. The sudden arrival in their midst of Japan's greatest general made them all realize that the big, decisive battle for the Philippines would not be long delayed.

Yamashita was up at four o'clock the next morning, inspect-ing the air defenses and ordering every unit to build deeper trenches. He was certain that the air attacks would get much heavier, and only Fort McKinley had a completely equipped underground air-defense system. Later in the day, he re-ported to Terauchi, whose headquarters had been moved to Manila six months before, and obtained approval for two important appointments.

He assumed that the first American invasion would come on Leyte, rather than on the principal island of Luzon. To command the 35th Army on Leyte, he appointed Lieutenant General Suzuki, who had been his chief of staff in Malaya. As his new chief of staff he selected Lieutenant General Akira Muto, who had replaced General Nishimura as com-mander of the Imperial Guards and was now with them in Sumatra. Muto wrote of his appointment:

In September, 1944, I saw a secret telegram saying that Yamashita had been appointed to command the Philip-pine Army. My view was that the appointment came six months too late—it was no use appointing a new com-mander at this time. When I received an order ten days later to join him as chief of staff, I knew that this was going to be my last service for my country. There is no general I would rather serve with than Yamashita, but I knew this appointment was a death sentence for me.

Within twenty-four hours of his arrival, Yamashita made

a very different impression upon his Headquarters from that of his predecessor. One officer reported it like this:

> Lunch was always called at twelve o'clock. There was a trumpet blast and the officers strolled along among the coconut palms to the mess. The custom in the Japanese Army is that junior officers do not begin to eat until the general takes up his chopsticks. The former commander would normally stroll in anything up to an hour late, in his shirt sleeves, wearing white golf stockings. No matter how hungry they were, the junior officers had to wait for him.
>
> The first day Yamashita took command, when the senior officers strolled into the mess they saw a big, burly man already eating rapidly from the rice bowl in his hand. It was some time before they realized this was their new general.

Another of Yamashita's innovations was to have the officers, after they had eaten, give him their reports while he sat finishing his rice.

He knew he had very little time and would not be able to reorganize his forces. As soon as Suzuki arrived, Yamashita sent him by plane to Leyte to make a defense plan. As it turned out, there was only a week in which to do it.

In Manila, Yamashita drew up his over-all battle plan, determining to fight the decisive conflict on Luzon. If the Americans landed on Leyte, Suzuki's forces must defend the island without reinforcements. While they fought a delaying battle, Yamashita would have time to regroup his forces on Luzon.

He knew he would finally lose the Philippines, but he was certain that if Suzuki could gain enough time, he would be able to make the final Luzon battle very costly, lengthy, and bloody for the Americans. Every day the war was prolonged would also give Japan more time to build up her mainland defenses.

Would he be able to carry out his plan? In the whole of the Philippines he had a total of 432,000 men—which was, incidentally, nearly twice as many as American intelligence had estimated. They included, however, a very large number of supply troops, and the Air Force, which was not under his command. On Luzon itself, he had 120,000 men. His total forces elsewhere numbered 100,000. There was also the 4th

Japanese Air Force, commanded by Lieutenant General Kyoji Tominaga, and 60,000 supply troops. In the Manila area were nearly 20,000 sailors and other naval forces.

Although he had plenty of troops, he had neither enough rice nor enough gasoline for a long campaign. As he remarked grimly: "If Leyte and Luzon are occupied by the American forces, they will accomplish it by hunger, not bullets."

Another ever-present problem was the attitude of the Filipinos. Soon after his arrival in Manila, Yamashita learned that the vast majority of them hated the Japanese. As he had pointed out already to the High Command in Tokyo, this was largely the fault of the Japanese. He fully realized that without the passive support of the Filipinos, or at least their neutrality, his task would be much more difficult.

He must keep them neutral—if he could. At this late stage, he believed the only way to do it was by threats. That is why he gave an interview to the press shortly after his arrival, in which he said: "Those who stand against the Japanese Army must be regarded as their enemies. In the Philippines today, the war has come to a situation of kill or be killed. No matter who the person is, a Filipino or not, if we hesitate, we ourselves will be killed."

There was no doubt that the guerrilla problem was very serious. The day he arrived in Manila, a mine, placed by Filipino partisans, exploded under the floor boards of his headquarters. American officers, landed by plane or submarine, were leading guerrilla troops who had been equipped with machine guns and other arms, superior in many cases to the Japanese armament. They were operating extensively in the main island of Luzon, and Yamashita was certain that as soon as the Americans landed, many more Filipinos would join them. His one aim was to frighten them off and keep the population as inactive as possible.

A few days after the Japanese commander arrived in Manila, an American amphibious fleet began to assemble in New Guinea and Honolulu. When the transports of this Third Amphibious Force met the American Seventh Fleet, the largest convoy ever seen in the Pacific started its voyage toward the Philippines.

The Japanese fleet was also active during the crucial days after the fall of Saipan. In the Formosa Strait, a force torpedoed the Australian heavy cruiser *Canberra* and the

American cruiser *Houston*. This action became tremendously exaggerated by the victory-hungry Japanese. They claimed they had either sunk or heavily damaged the astonishing total of fifty-seven American warships, including nineteen aircraft carriers. In celebration of this greatest overestimate of victory in the whole of the war, the Finance Ministry gave the entire population a free drink of sake. Their excitement was due mainly to the belief that an American attack would be delayed for at least two months, giving Yamashita time to perfect his defenses in the Philippines. It was on this occasion that Admiral Halsey of the American Third Fleet made his famous remark: "The ships reported by radio Tokyo as sunk have now been salvaged and are retiring toward the enemy."

In view of this "victory," Imperial Headquarters readily approved Yamashita's plan to have Suzuki bear the brunt of the first battle while his commander tried to make Luzon as impregnable as possible. They optimistically believed that Suzuki's force would not have much fighting, as the Japanese Air Force and Navy would be able to annihilate the Americans without too much trouble.

That was the confident mood of the Japanese High Command when the gigantic American convoy approached the Philippines. Two days before the fleet began to steam into Leyte Gulf, Japanese reconnaissance planes reported that large U. S. forces were approaching the islands. Still believing in their mythical destruction of the American aircraft carriers the Japanese reacted slowly. It was not until four days after the Americans had landed in strength that two hundred twin-engined bombers attacked them. By this time, the Americans were too strong for them and sixty-six Japanese planes were shot down.

On the afternoon in which the American fleet entered Leyte Gulf, General Suzuki gave his final defense orders to the 35th Army. He directed the 16th Division to meet and annihilate the American forces, and failing that, to stop them from making use of the Leyte airfield.

Next day, October 20, 1944, the quiet of the muggy tropical morning and the calm, glassy sea was shattered as the first shells from the American warships crashed among the palm trees and thatched huts of Leyte. Aircraft from the carriers swooped down to bomb the pillboxes along the coast where the 16th Division commander, General Makino, and his troops awaited the landings.

The only sign of Japanese activity was a reconnaissance plane, which disappeared after being fired on.

After two hours of bombardment, the troop transports began to edge inshore. Aboard them was the American 6th Army, commanded by General Walter Krueger, under orders to secure the airfields and naval bases near the coast in the Dulag and Tacloban areas. It was 10 A.M., when the first landing craft bounced over the smooth sea and slid onto the white coral beach.

The initial stages of the battle were strangely similar to the Japanese landings at Kota Bharu, in Malaya, at the beginning of the war. American troops scrambled up the beach under Japanese machine-gun and mortar fire. They captured two pillboxes, killing the eight Japanese defenders. Then they slowly pushed their way forward off the beach.

Just after midday, the tiny village of San José, with its palm-thatched huts, was in American hands. Under fire from Japanese pillboxes hidden in the swamps and flooded rice fields on either side the U. S. forces advanced along the road to the Tacloban airfield.

By midafternoon, the invaders had a sound beachhead, and transports and cargo ships were unloading rapidly. After lunch aboard the flagship, General MacArthur, the American Supreme Commander, waded ashore, accompanied by other generals and photographers. Standing on the beach, he made the statement that was to become well known. "I have returned. By the grace of Almighty God, our forces stand once again on Philippine soil." Then he uttered this rousing appeal to the embattled Filipinos:

As the lines of battle roll forward to bring you within the zones of operations, rise and strike. For your homes and hearts, strike. For future generations of your sons and daughters, strike. In the name of your sacred dead, strike. Let no arm be faint. Let every arm be steel.

The guidance of Divine God points the way. Follow in His name to the Holy Grail of righteous victory.

Then, before returning to the warship, he sat down under a palm tree and chatted for a time, while photographers took scores of pictures.

When the pictures of MacArthur were flashed around the world, General Yamashita made a grave miscalculation. He did not believe they were genuine. He thought they were mock-ups, prepared in New Guinea to be distributed as soon as the Americans landed on Leyte.

Later, he confessed ruefully: "If I had known that Mac-Arthur had been foolish enough, for the sake of a propaganda gesture, to land and sit under a palm tree in Leyte Gulf, I would have loosed the whole Japanese Air Force on him—if only to avenge the death of Admiral Yamamoto."

He was referring to Fleet Admiral Isoroku Yamamoto, who led the attack on Pearl Harbor. He was killed in April, 1943, by an American plane in Bougainville, in New Guinea. There is no doubt that this was a deliberate act of revenge. The Americans had cracked the Japanese secret cipher and were able to read a code message revealing the location of Yamamoto's plane.

By the end of their first day on Leyte, the U. S. forces had landed at several places along the coast and held a strong perimeter. It cost them 49 killed and 198 wounded.

What was the Japanese reaction? Still buoyed up by the mythical Formosa Strait victory, they were confident that the Americans would easily be thrown into the sea. In Yamashita's headquarters, they talked of demanding the surrender of the American forces after seizing General Mac-Arthur. It was noticeable that Yamashita, the master tactician, took no part in the optimistic discussions. He was, however, well satisfied that the Americans had landed on Leyte, as he had predicted they would, giving him much more time to prepare his defenses on Luzon.

Then he received a message that altered the conduct of the whole campaign. When the Americans landed on Leyte, Imperial Headquarters changed their minds. They canceled the plan to let Suzuki hold the island as long as he could without reinforcements while Yamashita got on with his main job of preparing the defenses of Luzon. Without warning, they sent a bombastic communication ordering all three armed forces to gather their power together and totally destroy the American forces on Leyte.

This order caused consternation at Yamashita's headquarters. His plan for a decisive battle on Luzon was not yet complete, nor were there enough reinforcements or transport for a major counterattack at Leyte.

His new chief of staff, Muto, had just arrived after a two-week journey from Sumatra to Manila. En route, he had been shot at by an American plane and had to crash-land, managing to jump clear just before his aircraft blew up. He reported covered with mud, his clothes in rags, and Yamashita had to lend him a uniform.

Muto's reception was just as ominous. While he was being introduced to his staff officers, there was a heavy air raid and they met crouching in a ditch. He was told that the Americans had just landed on Leyte.

"Very interesting," he commented. "Where is Leyte?"

He was soon to find out. His first job was to go with the commanding general to the official residence of Field Marshal Terauchi, where Yamashita pointed out that to obey the new orders would be a waste of precious time, effort, and men. It could only lead to the destruction of his Luzon defense plan and to final defeat. How could he supply munitions and food to the defenders of Leyte when he was so short of ships? The meeting lasted for two hours and officers outside the room could hear voices raised.

At last, Terauchi looked directly at Yamashita and said: "This is an order from our Emperor."

Yamashita, who had been expecting this, nodded and replied: "If our Emperor has consented to this plan, there is nothing else to do but proceed with it stubbornly."

Three days after the American landings, Yamashita ordered his first reinforcements to Leyte. The American advance was being resisted fiercely everywhere by Suzuki's troops, and the early stages of the invasion were marked by many savage battles fought between small forces in swamps and flooded fields, mostly in darkness.

Suzuki sent reinforcements to the nearby Burauen airfields where they built concealed pillboxes with coconut logs, and spiderholes—camouflaged pits about five feet deep, with a removable cover, just large enough to contain a man and his machine gun. When American tanks moved through the villages toward the airfield, Japanese jumped out of their spiderholes and hurled explosive charges against the vehicles blowing themselves up with them. As the tanks advanced through the flooded rice fields, they were fired on by Japanese hidden under village houses or in the tall grass.

In a typical battle, three companies of Japanese counterattacked down the road, supported by heavy mortar and machine-gun fire. They killed all the American troops they met until there was only one survivor. He was Private Harold

H. Moon, who, although badly wounded, threw grenades and held back the enemy for four hours, until dawn. Then a Japanese platoon charged him with fixed bayonets. Firing at them from a sitting position, he killed eighteen and repulsed the attack. When another machine gun opened up on his right, he tried to throw a grenade at it and was instantly killed. Private Moon was posthumously awarded the Medal of Honor.

Another ferocious little action took place when the Japanese raided a village. Pushing Filipinos in front of them, to make the American sentries think they were friendly guerrillas, they suddenly broke into the town square and threw grenades into houses, trucks, and a hospital, killing the wounded. The Japanese colonel who led the raid was killed before it was broken up.

In spite of this bitter fighting, within two weeks the American forces had secured the important airfields and roads in northern Leyte, and three weeks after the landings General MacArthur was able to announce, in a broadcast from the tiny provincial capital of Tacloban with its wooden coconut-thatched houses and unpaved streets, that civil government had been restored to the Philippines.

After the capture of Tacloban and the airfields, Suzuki planned to fall back into the mountains, taking with him enough ammunition and food for 20,000 men for six months. The Americans, however, had moved so quickly that they took the hills dominating the entire Leyte valley, so he concentrated his troops on the southern edge of the valley to await reinforcements.

Yamashita's troops were on their way, sailing into the port of Ormoc under fire from the American Air Force and Navy. The transports were attacked again and again by American planes, and four-fifths of them were sunk. As they hugged the coast, many of the troops were able to swim ashore, but they lost most of their equipment. In spite of these constant attacks, more than 45,000 troops and 10,000 tons of supplies were landed on Leyte. Although most of the tactical airfields were in the hands of the American 6th Army many of the landing strips were waterlogged and could not be put into service immediately.

Japanese estimates show that 10 per cent of their ships managed to regain port in Luzon. The smallest ships suffered the most; two-thirds of them were sunk on the way to Leyte and the remainder were destroyed on their way back. A convoy of one hundred ships sailed and only three came back. Those troops which managed to land on Leyte arrived with no weapons and only one-fifth of their food and ammunition. Altogether, seven thousand tons of rice left Luzon but only one thousand tons arrived; and as soon as it was landed, it was totally destroyed by an American air raid. Within a few weeks of the U. S. landings, the Japanese Army was on a starvation diet, subsisting chiefly on nuts and grass.

A Japanese staff officer reported: "Our soldiers are exhausted and ill from starvation. They have lost their will to fight and are staggering about in confusion with their communications broken down. I have seen any number of soldiers wandering around in the jungle on the edge of complete starvation, looking like ghosts."

One of the reinforcements that landed at Ormoc was the Japanese 1st Division, which, although without battle experience, was the best-equipped division in the Army. It had served in Manchuria during the China Incident and was transferred to Shanghai two months before the American invasion. Its appearance in the Philippines did a great deal for the morale of the Japanese troops there. The division's task was to spearhead a counterattack, though Yamashita had wanted to keep it to defend Luzon, he was forced to commit it to the Leyte battle.

Believing that with the 1st Division it would be easy to wipe out the U. S. forces and retake the airfields, Suzuki decided this was the time to counterattack and moved the division up the Ormoc valley in a ten-mile convoy. Assaulting it by land and air, the Americans soon realized that they were up against first-class troops. They lost thirty trucks and two tanks, and the U. S. Air Force reported that "very accurate ack-ack fire" had shot down two of their planes.

At this time the Americans had a bit of luck. On a dead Japanese officer they discovered Suzuki's plan for the big offensive which, spearheaded by the 1st Division, was to drive up the valley and retake the airfields. General Krueger quickly disposed his forces to meet the threat. The Japanese 1st Division dug themselves in at a place nicknamed Breakneck Ridge, and constructed a system of defensive log pillboxes and spiderholes from which the fire was so accurate that it could puncture the tires of American vehicles traveling along the road.

The American 24th Division was given the task of driving hem out. When the tanks clanked forward, Japanese jumped out of the tall grass and slapped magnetic mines against them. The battle was fought in continuous rain and thick mud, which was slippery and treacherous. Everywhere, the Japanese fought till they died. After each successful attack there remained isolated pockets of fierce resistance. To subdue pill-boxes still holding out against showers of grenades, the Americans poured gasoline down the ventilation pipes and ignited it, buring the defenders alive.

The U. S. troops, suffering from insufficient rations and broken sleep in sodden foxholes, were not much better off than the Japanese. There were many dead and wounded from the continual mortar and machine-gun fire and even more casualties from fever, dysentery, and foot ulcers.

The Japanese resistance was so fierce that it was four days before the American tanks were able to gain the crest of Breakneck Ridge, and not until two days later did all fighting cease. This encounter was expensive to both sides: it cost the Americans 630 men killed and wounded, but they counted 1,779 Japanese dead.

It was a month since the Americans had landed, and both sides now realized that the struggle for the island of Leyte was going to be far longer and costlier than they had anticipated. Yamashita held a two-day conference with Field Marshal Terauchi, strongly advising him that the Leyte operation should be discontinued. He said that it was now obvious that no more Japanese reinforcements would reach the Philippines and that all their vital manpower was needed for the defense of Luzon, rather than being wasted at Leyte. Yamashita produced charts showing that transport and naval ships were getting scarcer every day and that the transportation of troops to Leyte was becoming impossible. Suzuki's land operations, he also admitted, were not "proceeding as favorably as they should."

Terauchi, however, was unmoved by the arguments and insisted that the battle be continued—and won. It was a direct order, and Yamashita rose and bowed, saying: "I fully understand your intention. I will try and carry the campaign out to a successful end."

As they left, Muto muttered: "The old man expects a miracle victory. He believes he will get help from Heaven."

It was their last conference with Terauchi. A week later—

only six months after he had transferred his headquarters to Manila from Singapore—the Field Marshal removed to Saigon, where he had begun the war. He always said he liked to "keep his operational post like the hinge of a fan so he could swing in any direction." There was undisguised relief at his departure.

Meanwhile, General Krueger was not pleased with the slow progress of his troops. There was no doubt that Yamashita's men were much fiercer, more determined soldiers in man-to-man battles. Krueger thought his own troops were too road-bound. Often, small resistance on a highway held up a whole division. Swamps, jungles, and flooded rice fields made it perilous to leave the road, but he was aware that the Japanese constantly waded into these areas and stayed there to fight. The general's complaint was that even if they encountered minor resistance, the Americans fell back, calling for artillery and mortar fire. Very often, the pounding of heavy artillery and mortars gave warning of a coming attack and enabled the Japanese to inflict heavy casualties on the Americans. A typical incident occurred when a company called for the shelling of a roadblock and then withdrew three hundred yards as it began. When the fire lifted and they returned to the roadblock, the Japanese had got back there first.

General Krueger need not have worried. The mortaring and shelling were very effective. Colonel Junkichi Okabayashi, chief of staff of the Japanese 1st Division, estimated the losses sustained by his troops as follows: 60 per cent from artillery, 25 per cent from mortars, and only 14 per cent from infantry fighting.

While fierce hand-to-hand fighting went on, the staff officers on both sides made many silly mistakes. The information on Suzuki's proposed offensive found on a dead officer was not an isolated incident. Japanese officers made no attempt to destroy identification papers before going into battle. Many of them carried orders and battle maps in their pockets.

The Americans were just as careless. Over San Francisco radio, they broadcast many accurate accounts of the battles before reports from Japanese front-line units reached 35th Army Headquarters. The Japanese on Leyte constantly monitored the American radio and found its information so useful that they were often able to prepare battle plans from it.

By this time, each side was able to size up its enemy. The American view of the Japanese was that their attacks were well conceived but were not mounted with enough troops. Also, units did not receive their orders and did not reach their appointed place in time. The Japanese, however, were well trained and led by officers with a strong sense of duty. As long as one officer remained alive, even the smallest force was still capable of savage fighting. The Japanese felt that the American Army had overwhelming striking power and that its operations were planned in minute detail and carried out scrupulously.

This was the position when another Japanese division— the 26th—landed at Ormoc after a rough voyage from Manila, during which they were under constant air attack. They came in three large transports escorted by destroyers, but many landing barges ran aground on the voyage. Most of their ammunition and provisions were left behind on the ships, which were so heavily bombarded in Ormoc harbor that they had to put out to sea to avoid being sunk. The 26th Division, assigned to defend Ormoc, fought a savage battle with the Americans for a week. Then a new U. S. division—the 77th— landed just below Ormoc and the Japanese unit was trapped. The fall of Ormoc was now only a matter of time.

Yamashita sent a staff officer to contact Suzuki and find out what was happening. He could not go by air, as he would almost certainly have been shot down; it took him three days' travel in a small ship to reach Ormoc from Luzon, moving at night and hiding in little inlets in the daytime. This is what he reported:

The skyline is full of American ships and the city of Ormoc is a ruin of stone and steel with no living thing, not even a cat to be seen. There is a constant crash of explosives among the ruined houses. Bodies are strewn along the roadside, burned black like statues, their rotting faces covered with flies. There is a terrible smell from these and from the many bodies of soldiers, all swollen up, and floating among the transports.

I found General Suzuki had transferred fifteen miles away along the coast toward the mountains. As I traveled along the road, I found the situation very bad. All the soldiers were on the verge of starvation. They were just skin and bone and looked like living corpses. They had very few weapons among them. They cannot communicate with other units and have lost their will to fight. They certainly have no strength to put in a counterattack. A senior staff officer had procured some whiskey from somewhere and was always drunk. Somehow, this sight shocked me more than all the horrors.

In spite of the gloomy report this officer carried back to Yamashita, the Japanese in Ormoc were still capable of savage fighting. American troops encountered little resistance on the outskirts of the town, but they soon came to a deep ravine where the enemy was dug in. They had to use grenades and mortars and finally bayonets to dislodge him.

This is an American view of the end of Ormoc:

The town is a blazing inferno of bursting white phosphorus shells, burning houses and exploding ammunition dumps. Over it all hangs a pall of heavy smoke mixed with the gray dust of blown-up buildings. Although the Japanese have been forced to retreat from the town, many are left behind and they heroically but hopelessly fight to delay the American advance. They are hidden in spiderholes under the buildings and the American infantry have to clear the town, street by street.

When it was realized that the reinforcement port of Ormoc was lost, Yamashita was faced with an impossible situation. In spite of this, the High Command stubbornly insisted that the battle must go on. Their view was that if the American land-based air strength on Leyte increased any more, the lines of communication between the Philippines and Japan would be completely severed.

They therefore devised a desperate plan to recapture the Leyte airfields.

CHAPTER 9

The Heavenly Troops

There was no doubt that if the Japanese could wrench back control of the Leyte airfields, it would greatly assist their 35th Army, which was reeling under the massive American attack.

Yamashita sent this order to General Suzuki: "If construction of the air bases in Leyte is permitted to continue, communication with the homeland wll be cut. This will be a serious situation, so we must occupy the Burauen airfields as soon as possible. At the same time, we must neutralize Tacloban and Dulag airfields. We must annihilate the enemy's air power."

Every available Japanese soldier who could be used was included in the operation. Battered remnants of units on Leyte were ordered over the mountain ranges to attack the airfields simultaneously with the landing of parachutists and suicide troops.

There was great opposition to this plan. Many staff officers felt that it was asking men to die in a hopeless attack. Yamashita replied: "I fully understand the opposition to the plan, but Suzuki was my chief of staff in Malaya and he and his men cannot be allowed to die without our doing something for them. If we can drive the U. S. forces off the airfields, it will give us more time to plan our next battle."

It was decided that demolition experts, protected by a

special detachment of Formosan soldiers recruited from head-hunters, and airborne suicide troops would undertake the main attack. Some of the suicide troops carried only swords as weapons. Their first task was to land heavy bombers with their wheels up to block the runways.

A preliminary force to test the American defenses left Manila in three air transports at night. At three o'clock the next morning, they were seen with their lights on, flying over Leyte Gulf at an altitude of about fifty feet. One of them crashed-landed offshore near some American troops, who assumed it was a friendly plane and climbed on the wing to offer assistance. More than twenty Japanese jumped out and threw grenades at them. Two Japanese were shot before the rest ran along the beach and disappeared into a swamp.

A second aircraft crashed on another beach and all the Japanese escaped. A third plane did land on Buri airstrip with its wheels up, but all its occupants were killed.

The operation was a complete failure but the Japanese radio and newspapers, still victory-hungry, claimed it was a great success. They called the troops "God's soldiers" because they dropped down from heaven. In any case, the Japanese were flogging a dead horse in trying to capture the fields. The day before the airborne attack, the three main airstrips on Leyte had been abandoned. There had been an inch of rain a day for forty days, and flooding had made them unusable, so the Americans had decided to build other landing strips with better drainage, in a different area.

Unaware of this, Yamashita was perfecting details of a much more elaborate and desperate plan to retake the airfields. General Makino's 16th Division, which had fought the Americans in the first Leyte battle was ordered to infiltrate through the mountains toward Buri airfield in the north. The 26th Division, which was still fighting on the shores of Ormoc Bay, was told to move over the mountains to attack Bayug and San Pablo, the southern airstrips. If all went well, they were to combine and move on to capture the Dulag field, on the shores of Leyte Gulf. On the night of December 5, the ground troops were to be in position, waiting for a big airborne landing, after which both groups would attack simultaneously.

Unfortunately for Yamashita, this plan was known to the Americans because the Japanese had once again gone into action carrying secret information. Documents taken off parachutists killed in the first raid indicated that they were only the vanguard of a big coordinated ground and airborne attack. Acting upon this information, American patrols blocked all known trails leading over the mountains toward the airstrips. They did not believe, however, that the enemy was capable of launching a major attack in the Burauen area. They were only partially correct.

General Suzuki moved with his troops into the mountains near Burauen to take charge of the attack, leaving his deputy, General Yoshiharu Tomochika, in command of the Ormoc battle.

Suzuki asked that the attack be postponed to give him a little more time to prepare for it, but Yamashita would agree only to its being put off one day—until December 6. This was to lead to great confusion. The 26th Division received orders on the change of date; but because of radio difficulties, the 16th did not. Right on time, on December 5, remnants of the 16th Division came down from the mountains, heading for Buri airfield. There were only five hundred of them and their morale was very low. They had been living on coconuts and bananas, their officers having taken the few remaining rations. They had also been forced to leave their wounded in the mountains.

As they made their way down a jungle trail, they ran into the waiting Americans and suffered two hundred casualties from artillery and tanks. The survivors hid in a deep gorge, three miles away from the airstrip, ready to move out and join the paratroopers in the attack. Unaware that the plan had been postponed for twenty-four hours, 150 of them made a dawn attack on the airstrip, which was manned by two hundred American troops, mostly engineering and signal units. The Japanese charged into the American camp and bayoneted men asleep in their blankets. Naked Americans jumped out of bed, grabbed their weapons, and fired on them. The Japanese then fell back and entrenched themselves in a wood on the edge of the field.

That evening forty transports, carrying one thousand parachutists, left Manila. Accompanied by bombers and fighters, they roared over the Burauen airfields just after dark. Only sixteen managed to land, many of the others having been destroyed by ground artillery.

Meanwhile, incendiary bombs were dropped on the San Pablo strip, setting a gasoline dump on fire, and three hundred parachutists began to descend in the light from the flames. They burned planes on the ground and set fire to gasoline and ammunition dumps. Then they began attacking barracks and communications. A confused battle marked by uncontrolled and disorganized firing raged all night. At dawn, the American Air Corps troops retreated in a hurry, abandoning rifles, machine guns, grenades, and ammunition. The Japanese seized these and joined the remaining men of the 16th Division on Buri airstrip, where only sixty paratroopers had been dropped.

Next morning, two American battalions were ordered to Buri, but they were held up by a rain-swollen swamp which they had to wade through; in some places it was shoulder-deep. They did not arrive until dusk and were immediately fired on by the Japanese machine-gunners.

Three days later, while the men of the Japanese 16th Division were still attacking strongly, a battalion of the 26th—the only one to arrive—reached the airfield. Disorganized, hungry, and tired, the men were not much use in the battle and were easily driven back by the Americans.

That evening, the Japanese launched a final fierce attack, using captured weapons, and pushed the Americans off the perimeter. It was their last effort. The U. S. troops rallied and in a savage thrust, drove their enemy from the airstrip. The Japanese disappeared into the jungle, leaving thirty dead behind them.

Nevertheless, the parachutists and ground troops had done much better on Buri than on the other strips. The transports due to land on Tacloban had been shot down by antiaircraft guns. Others crash-landed at Dulag, killing all their occupants. The much-vaunted heavenly soldiers had failed completely.

What was their final score? They had destroyed fuel and supply dumps and some American planes; they had also held Buri airfield for five days—but their attempt to wrest the initiative from the Americans had not succeeded.

Realizing this and worried about mounting American pressure in the Ormoc area, Suzuki ordered all operations against the Burauen airfields to be discontinued and the troops to return to the Ormoc valley.

It was not an easy journey. A Japanese staff officer who made the march wrote:

When Suzuki went into the mountains, every walkable

track was occupied by guerrillas, who fired on the Japanese. We had to fight our way through the jungle, which was very thick. Even in daytime it was dark and damp, and at night there were many leeches. Although it was only a short distance, it took a long time.

Then the rain came. It was intensely cold and the men's teeth began to chatter. They could not light a match to make tea because it was so damp.

When we got to the high mountains, the paths were so steep and the men were so tired that they could not lift a leg to step over a corpse. They just fell over it and staggered on.

No one could sleep because of the cold. No one spoke in the daytime. They just walked along, dumb, suffering from fatigue and starvation, dragging their numb legs along. They were like sleepwalkers, trudging along to keep themselves warm. Rotten trees gave off an eerie phosphoresence which guided the soldiers a little.

At the end of this march, Suzuki said to me: "You'd better get back to Manila as soon as possible and tell Yamashita I am very sorry but the Leyte action is going very badly."

This was the condition of the troops retreating over the mountains when Imperial Headquarters released this communique: "Our forces are still holding the Burauen airfields and are fighting fiercely on the mountains near Ormoc."

Actually Leyte was lost and Suzuki's army was rapidly disintegrating. Wounded men were sent back into the front line, but many of them refused to fight. Desertion was common. All the troops were starving. The famous 1st Division was finished. It had exhausted its food and ammunition and the troops were eating coconuts, grass, bamboo shoots, and coconut fiber. Many of them vomited several times a day because they could not digest this unpalatable food.

If a man was badly wounded, there were no longer any proper facilities for medical treatment. Officers went around asking the wounded to commit suicide. General Tomochika, chief of staff of the 35th Army, stated: "This was particularly common among soldiers of the elite 1st Division. However, the majority died willingly. Only the Japanese could have done such a thing—and yet I could not bear to see it."

Southern Region Headquarters in Saigon were now completely out of touch and unrealistic about the losing battle in the Philippines. Terauchi sent his chief of operations, Lieutenant General Jo Iimura, with a message saying: "The 14th Army Group will continue to attack the enemy forces at Leyte while at the same time the defenses at Luzon should be strengthened."

While Yamashita was pondering on how to deal with this foolish message, the Americans landed on another Philippine island, Mindoro. This changed the situation so much for the worse that he was able to convince General Iimura that every resource must be used to defend Luzon alone.

Iimura agreed and flew back to Saigon with Yamashita's amended plan. When Marshal Terauchi learned what his chief of operations had done, he immediately transferred him to a nonoperational command, the almost defunct 2nd Army in the East Indies.

Having finally obtained agreement to his original plan, Yamashita had to break the news to Suzuki that the Leyte campaign must be written off. On Christmas Day, he sent him the following message:

Sixty days have elapsed since the Americans invaded Leyte Island, during which period the 35th, under the forceful leadership of its commander, has waged many and heroic battles against superior enemy forces. I am deeply impressed with the units which captured the enemy airfields at Burauen. I cannot keep back tears for the tens of thousands of officers and men fighting on Leyte Island.

Nevertheless, I must impose a still harder task upon you. They say it is harder to live than to die. You must be patient enough to endure the hardships of life and help to maintain the prosperity of the Imperial Throne. Be ready to meet your death calmly for our beloved country.

Not everyone was anxious to die. There were many deserters who built boats and set out for small neighboring islands. One of them was Lieutenant General Shimpei Fukue, commander of the 102nd Division. Suzuki, who had not heard from him for some time, found he was planning to sail off to the island of Cebu. He sent a message stating that Fukue was "violating the military code in taking these steps without consent," and ordered the divisional commander to report to him in person.

Fukue did not obey the summons. He sent a reply which said simply: "The divisional commander is so busy preparing for retreat that he is unable to report to Army H.Q." When Suzuki heard this, he flew into such a rage that a Japanese staff officer noted: ". . . for several days, everyone had a difficult time calming the General."

Suzuki removed General Fukue from his command and asked Imperial Headquarters for authority to court-martial him, but he received no reply. Eventually, he was forced to restore Fukue to command.

In spite of these difficulties, Suzuki tried hard to obey Yamashita's orders to make his troops as self-supporting as possible. He told them to plant sweet potatoes and Indian corn. They also acquired large quantities of coconuts and rice from the Filipinos. They obtained salt from the sea and ate jungle ferns, grass, and wild spinach as vegetables.

But as there were still too many soldiers on Leyte for the food supply, Suzuki decided to transfer his best remaining fighting troops to the neighboring islands of Cebu and Mindanao. Hundreds of Japanese troops left for the islands in launches, but after the evacuation had been underway for a week, it was spotted by American aircraft, and PT boats and planes stopped further movement. Only 750 men had managed to cross to Cebu. There were still 20,000 Japanese on Leyte, but for two months it was impossible to move any of them to other islands.

Then, one evening, two small launches carrying General Suzuki and his staff sailed from Leyte and reached Cebu. A month later, Suzuki was killed by an American bomber while enroute to Mindanao in a small sailboat.

The records of the Leyte battle show that the Americans lost 3,500 killed and 12,000 wounded. General Tomochika, Suzuki's chief of staff estimated that there were 61,800 Japanese troops on the island when the Americans landed. On the day Suzuki sailed to Mindanao, only 13,010 were still alive. Most of them had died of diseases and starvation rather than wounds.

The attempt to send reinforcements and supplies to Leyte had seriously crippled the fighting power of Yamashita's forces. The once formidable Japanese Air Force was "transformed into a sacrificial army of guided missiles." In other words, they were now completely dependent upon suicide pilots.

Yamashita's verdict was: "After our losses in Leyte, I realized that I could no longer fight a decisive battle for the Philippines."

CHAPTER 10

The Battle No One Wanted

Yamashita was back at last to his original plan: to fight the main battle on Luzon—and make it for the Americans as costly, bloody, and prolonged as possible. When he had been ordered to send reinforcements to Leyte, he knew his hopes must end for any sort of victory in the Philippines. Following the Leyte disaster, an atmosphere of defeat hung over his headquarters. He had had 120,000 fighting troops in Luzon, but 30,000 of his best soldiers had been sent to Leyte, leaving him with 90,000 for the defense of the main island in the Philippines.

Some reinforcements had come from Japan—the 23rd, 10th, and 19th divisions—but they had lost a third of their officers and most of their equipment on the voyage as a result of attacks by American planes and submarines. Once the invasion forces reached Luzon, Yamashita felt sure he could expect no more reinforcements; Imperial Headquarters would write off Luzon as a strategic loss.

The battle was not going to be easy. His greatest problem was food. Although the Philippines was an agricultural country, it had always imported much food from abroad. During the Japanese occupation, it had received rice from Indo-china and Thailand. Now this was cut off. Imperial Head-quarters promised to send rations, but everyone knew that in the present situation there was no hope of their arriving. In fact, only one shipment of rice arrived safely during the eleven months of Yamashita's command.

His chief of staff, Muto, made this comment later: "At the end of December, 1944, Manila Bay was untenable for Japanese shipping. No ships could get in or out owing to the severity of the air and submarine attack."

Much of the rice harvested in Luzon had been sent to Leyte. A month after the Leyte landings, the Japanese soldier's ration was cut from three pounds a day to less than one pound.

Another problem was transportation. The roads and railroads in Luzon, once the finest transportation system in the Pacific outside Japan, had been allowed to fall into ruin during General Kuroda's regime. Muto reported that they were "in a shocking state of disrepair," and many main roads had been destroyed by guerrilla action.

The Army had 4,600 vehicles, but half of them were damaged. There was little gasoline, and distilled pine-root oil was used as a substitute. Munitions were also short, because they had either been sent to Leyte or lost in transit.

The Japanese were short of food, fuel, ammunition, and transport—everything that an army needs to ensure victory. No matter how heroic the soldiers, how brilliant the field commanders, how shrewd and experienced the general— without these supplies, defeat was certain.

Yamashita, however, was fully aware that he had one priceless weapon in his hand. It was a weapon that anyone who fought against the Japanese in World War II will never deny. It was his faithful, fanatic troops—the finest infantry in the world. On a bowl of rice and a strip of dried fish, these men would fight like a pride of lions. Yamashita understood these fighting men well. He knew he would shortly ask them to undertake the impossible. Even men like these cannot fight forever with no hope of reinforcement, with their daily food dwindling inexorably to nothing. But the men would not fail him; rather, it was he and the Japanese High Command who were about to fail them.

He turned from soldiers and supplies to the conduct of the battle. Knowing he could not defend the whole of Luzon, he decided to abandon the central plains in the Manila Bay area and concentrate his forces on three mountain strongholds. These could be overrun only at great cost in time and American lives. Minor delaying tactics by isolated units would be undertaken at other points. The main plan was to hold the approaches of the Cagayan valley, one of the greatest food-producing areas in the Philippines, until it could be stripped of every grain of rice and other food for his mountain fortresses.

Another place he abandoned was Lingayen Gulf. He had little doubt that the Americans would attack there; it was the classic and logical landing place, and the Japanese had used it in their invasion of the Philippines in 1941. It had very good beaches of firm sand and behind it was the road and rail system of Luzon.

On the other hand, he was fully aware that the massive American forces building up on Leyte could select a hundred other landing points and he could not prevent their getting a foothold. Once they had landed, their strength, fire power, and mobility would lead only to useless massacres if his troops tried to fight them on the plains near Lingayen Gulf or the flat rice lands of Luzon. Instead, he could cause much greater damage and more casualties by a long-drawn-out delaying action in the hills.

His battle plan did not include the defense of Manila, the Philippine capital. His view was that Manila's only value lay in its harbor, the finest in the Pacific, and airfield; if these were destroyed, there would be no further point in fighting for the city. Other reasons for not defending the capital were: (1) it was impossible to feed the million inhabitants; (2) most of the buildings were very inflammable; and (3) Manila was built on flat land and would need at least eight divisions to defend it, which was much more strength than he could spare.

To control the battle, he planned to move his headquarters to Baguio, the cool and beautiful Philippine summer capital, five thousand feet up in the mountains. Lieutenant General Shizuo Yokoyama was left with a strong force south of Manila; his orders were not to defend the capital but to keep troops there long enough to cover the evacuation of supplies and delay the Americans by the demolition of roads and bridges. Manila had been a Japanese Army base for three years and there were many equipment, munitions, and food dumps within the city limits.

Yamashita's decision to abandon Manila was greatly resented by the Japanese admirals and the 4th Air Army commander, Lieutenant General Tominaga. The naval units were under the command of Vice Admiral Denshichi Okochi, who took his orders directly from Tokyo Naval Headquarters.

His most important shore-based naval unit was the 31st Special Base Force, commanded by Rear Admiral Sanji Iwabachi.

When Field Marshal Terauchi's headquarters moved back to Saigon from Manila, steps were taken to try to unify the Philippine command. Yet it was not until January 1, 1945, that Yamashita was given control of the 4th Air Army, which by then had hardly any planes left. He never had any naval control.

The Navy, which always made a feature of cooperating as little as possible with Japanese generals, completely ignored Yamashita's withdrawal plans. Their view was that if Manila was abandoned without a fight, the defense of Luzon would be meaningless. General Tominaga agreed with them and refused to provide any help in preparing defenses outside the capital. Instead he helped in the Navy preparations, concealing his troops in the woods around the city.

Yamashita had had trouble with Tominaga from the first. He was a friend of Tojo's and had been Assistant War Minister in Tokyo. It was he who had launched the parachutists and suicide pilots on their ill-fated attacks on the Leyte airfield. He was responsible for the formation of the kamikaze—"divine wind"—suicide pilots into regular units. These human-bomb flyers had been used first by the Navy to attack American warships. But as planes became scarce, Tominaga formed his Air Force into regular suicide squadrons, who took off on scheduled death missions. He was noted for the eloquence of his farewell speeches to the kamikaze pilots before they took off on their journey of no return. He had a set speech, which he delivered more than sixty times:

When men decide to die like you, they can move the heart of the Emperor. And I can assure you the death of every one of you will move the Emperor. It will do more —it will even change the history of the world.

I know what you feel now as you put the sorrows and joys of life behind you because the Emperor's fortunes are failing. Do not worry about what happens when you die and what you leave behind you—for you will become gods. Soon I hope to have the privilege of joining you in glorious death.

In spite of the opposition, Yamashita continued with his

plan. He ordered that 70,000 tons of supplies be moved out of the city before the Americans arrived. Then he found that with his existing transports it would take six months to move it all. The orders were revised: 13,000 tons of the most vital supplies were to be taken out by mid-January. When the Americans landed, on January 9, 1945, only 4,000 tons had been shifted.

Yamashita also ordered all Japanese women and children in Luzon to return home as soon as possible. There were a large number of Japanese girls working at military head-quarters in Manila. Some were residents of the Philippines, but others had come from Japan with the Army. Most of them wanted to remain to the last, but Yamashita insisted that they go home.

He ran into difficulties even with this humane scheme. It had been decided in Tokyo that no Japanese women and children should be repatriated, because if the Japanese saw them arriving, the real state of the war would leak out to the public. The government felt this might weaken their fighting spirit. Acting upon government instructions, the Japanese consul in Manila rejected Yamashita's plan, but the general told him: "I know the real state of the battle. It is a very grave moment and I will take responsibility for their repatriation."

When the women and children boarded the troopship that would take them home, he sent Muto to see them off with this message: "When you return to Japan, you must become good wives and mothers." But not all the Japanese service girls left on this ship. Once again, the Navy and Air Force opposed Yamashita, refusing to send their girls back to Japan. Tominaga insisted on keeping his girls as "consola-tion" for the suicide units. Other girls deserted and secretly attached themselves to units. The result was that all the Army girls went home, but the Navy and Air Force girls remained.

Another difficulty arose concerning the 1,300 U. S. pris-oners and 7,000 interned civilians on Luzon. Because of the shortage of food and transport, the Japanese Army could not move them out of Manila, so Yamashita ordered that when the Americans landed on Luzon, these prisoners should be handed over to them and a list of their names supplied to the protecting power. When he reported this action to South-ern Region Headquarters in Saigon, they answered that in their view it was far too early to free prisoners. Yamashita refused to change his orders, replying that he was the best judge of the most suitable time.

Yamashita and his staff left Manila on Christmas Eve, choosing that time because they thought the American forces would be celebrating the holiday. On New Year's Day, he was still at his temporary headquarters, a small hut near the banks of the Manila dam. After he and Muto prayed for the Emperor and drank a little rice wine, they spent the rest of the day planning their defense against the coming invasion.

On January 2, he began to move his headquarters up to Baguio, the summer resort with its white-painted houses with red roofs and the tower of the Catholic church peeping through the green pines. Before leaving, he ordered General Yokoyama, commanding the Manila rear guard, not to force his men to die in suicide attacks, as this would not deter the enemy. He estimated that the American attack would come within three weeks. He was wrong; only a week after he arrived in Baguio, the invasion fleet appeared off the shores of Luzon.

Field Marshal Terauchi had arranged to send to Lingayen Gulf 10,000 tons of rice and 10,000 drums of gasoline. Yamashita sent two of his reinforcement units, the 19th and 23rd Divisions, which had recently arrived from Korea, to help unload the stores, but the supply ships never arrived. They had all been sunk by warships guarding the American invasion fleet. Had the supplies been successfully delivered, it would have made a great difference to the Japanese.

The next morning, hundreds of American ships appeared on the horizon. When one Japanese staff officer, observing through a telescope, tried to count them, there were so many that he gave up. Muto remarked ruefully: "We expected rice. We got the American Army instead."

The Americans began to shell the Japanese 19th and 23rd Divisions, who were hiding among the coconut and mango trees and thatched huts on the shore. Having learned a great deal from the Leyte invasion, Tominaga's Air Force unit and the Navy reacted very quickly. They put in heavy kamikaze attacks, which damaged many American battleships and also the heavy cruiser *Australia,* forcing it to withdraw from the battle.

The importance of these attacks was not so much in the great damage they did as in the psychological effect they created. The kamikaze assaults were relatively small because the Japanese had not completely organized their suicide force but they were pressed home with such ferocity that the morale of the invading troops was badly shaken. Unfortunately for the Japanese, they did not realize the devastating effect the kamikaze planes were having upon the Americans. If they had been able to mass two hundred aircraft in a single concentrated suicide attack, the invasion of Luzon might have been a very different story.

The U. S. warships continued their fierce bombardment. Many Japanese soldiers were burned to death when ammunition dumps were hit by the shells. Then the Americans began to land with tanks, self-propelled guns, and flame throwers. They met very little opposition other than that of some Japanese fanatics who put white towels around their heads—the feudal symbol that they were preparing to die— and charged the American lines with hand grenades, blowing themselves up. U. S. planes added to the inferno as they continually bombed the Japanese positions.

Under an unceasing hail of shells and bombs, the defenders fell back little by little. They tried to take shelter in the nearby woods, but the Americans dropped phosphorus bombs that set the trees on fire. Soon the only battle tactic left to the Japanese was to hold on during the daytime as best they could and counterattack at night.

The thin armor of the Japanese light tanks was easily penetrated by the U. S. fire, while their own shells bounced off the heavy American tanks, inflicting little damage, and the big vehicles began to roll over the foxholes, as the Japanese soldiers said, "like heavy rollers crushing eggs."

Fierce hand-to-hand fighting developed, in which Japanese officers fought with their long samurai swords. Other troops, their weapons destroyed, threw rocks at the Americans.

Realizing that this was the main thrust—the long-expected assault on Luzon—Yamashita warned his commanders that they must be self-sufficient in food and other materials, as the battle would undoubtedly become so fierce that they would be unable to receive outside assistance. He issued an order which made clear his lack of equipment: "It is easy to die with honor but it is much more difficult to hold up the enemy advance when you are short of ammunition and food. Those of you in the front line will be doing your duty if you hold them up for a day—or even half a day."

A very different kind of order came from Southern Region Headquarters in Saigon, exhibiting the usual unrealistic view: "The enemy has made his advance far into our line. We must destroy him in one battle."

Many of the Japanese war correspondents with Yamashita noted how serious he looked. One man wrote: "He has the air of a man about to fight his last battle." Another noted in his diary: "Here on these islands in the vast Pacific Ocean a great tragedy is about to occur." "When the news came," wrote another correspondent, "I knew that Luzon would be our last battle. But since I have seen Yamashita, I know I will be glad to die with him in honor. If people could only see the way he is conducting this battle, the fighting spirit would rise in Japan. Our only hope in Japan is to depend on the Tiger of Malaya's somehow making a success."

Yamashita sent a messenger to Tokyo with a full report of the American invasion. He also directed him to take a note to Mrs. Yamashita in Kamakura, which said: "Please discuss with my elder brother the matter of taking Kumiyo into our family. If there are any documents, you can send them to me by courier from Japan to the Philippines." He added a word about the campaign: "The American Army has landed and is already at my knee but everyone is in good spirits. We are brave enough to deal them a heavy blow but our main difficulty is ammunition. I may be silent for some time as I am very busy."

It was the last letter she received from him. But she did what he asked. She arranged for him to adopt his brother's son as his own.

Meanwhile, his headquarters in Baguio were now under heavy air attack. The two base hospitals there were so badly damaged that everyone was evacuated, except the most seriously wounded. Some nurses volunteered to stay with them. Then an American raid burned the whole city down, including the hospitals and school. All the nurses and patients who had remained were killed.

Anticipating these air raids, Yamashita had ordered dug into the hillside a tunnel eight hundred yards long. Here he could work without interruption from bombs. Conditions in the tunnel were far from pleasant. No one could leave it during daylight because of the bombing, and it was lit by lamps using pine-root oil. The fumes and the temperature were so bad that now and again people would stagger half-suffocated to the entrance to gulp some fresh air. As they stood there "gasping like goldfish," as one officer described it, all they could see remaining of the once beautiful city of Baguio was the bomb-damaged steeple of the Catholic church.

Most of the hospital patients had been taken to a mine, the shaft of which was two miles long. At one time, there were six hundred people in this mine. Nurses and orderlies used ore cars to carry patients and bandages along the galleries. This improvised underground hospital was damp and airless, and water poured from the ceiling. Hundreds of badly wounded soldiers lay moaning on the floor, while nurses groped around in the semidarkness, slipping on blood and trying to look after the patients as best they could. The smell and the noise were horrible. Some men raved in delirium; others kept groaning, "Please kill me!"

This was the position in Baguio when the Americans burst out onto the plains and cut communications between Yamashita and his troops fighting there. At the same time, he received two shocks from his own forces. The first concerned General Tominaga, the Air Force commander. As nearly all his planes had been destroyed and he had hardly any gasoline left, he was supposed to put in a few more suicide attacks, then turn his troops into infantry to help Yamashita in the defense battle in the mountains. Instead, this general, who had made such inspiring speeches about soon joining his men in the glory of death, ran away.

A pilot came to Yamashita with the following message: "The commander of the 4th Air Force, Tominaga, has decided it is useless for him to remain in the Philippines with no planes and no gasoline." Without asking Yamashita's permission, he had taken one of his last planes and flown to Formosa. Yamashita lost his temper completely and delivered a furious tirade to the messenger, who stood at attention.

In spite of his preoccupation with the American invasion, Yamashita was determined to have Tominaga court-martialed. He sent many messages to Tokyo and Saigon, but Tominaga was a friend of Tojo and other well-placed persons in Japan and Yamashita was never able to make an example of him. In fact, Tominaga received only a slight reduction in rank and was posted as a divisional commander to Manchuria. When the Red Army invaded Manchuria during the last few days of World War II, Tominaga was captured. Many years later, he was still in a labor camp in Siberia.

The silence which followed the American break-through onto the plains ended when a message arrived from Navy Headquarters, stating that U. S. forces had arrived on the outskirts of Manila and the Japanese were heavily engaging them. This was the first news that the battle for the city, which Yamashita had not wanted and had, indeed, expressly forbidden, had begun. It would last a month and prove to be one of the most savage conflicts of the war, more bitter and barbaric than the siege of Stalingrad.

Neither army commander wanted the battle. MacArthur broadcast an appeal to make Manila an open city. In many ways this coincided with Yamashita's own views, but he had no power to act on it. It was a matter for Tokyo Headquarters, which, on the advice of the admirals and the Air Force commander, refused to agree. The battle was entirely the result of the obstinacy of the Japanese admirals and Tominaga, who had deserted to Formosa a fortnight before it began.

Yamashita had no intention of being responsible for the destruction of Manila. He had evacuated troops and supplies, leaving a small army to maintain order and blow the bridges over the Pasig River, to delay the American advance. General Yokoyama had been commanded to quit the city as speedily as possible, once he had concluded his demolition.

But as the Army units pulled out of the city, naval troops moved in, revealing for the last and most tragic time what could result from the disunity of Japan's separate commands. Admiral Okochi, commander of the Southwest Area Fleet and the highest-ranking naval officer in the Philippines, decided on his own initiative that Manila was a natural fortress which should not be weakly abandoned without a struggle but rather defended at great cost to the Americans. He nominated Rear Admiral Iwabachi, commanding a force of 15,000–16,000 naval troops, not only to destroy all naval installations but to fight for the city.

Iwabachi misled Yamashita by insisting that the Navy's only reason for remaining in Manila was to destroy or defend naval facilities there. Assuming they would retire from the city later, according to plan, Yamashita urged Iwabachi to strengthen the defenses of Fort McKinley and set up an alternative headquarters outside Manila. But Iwabachi was determined to defend Manila with every man and every piece of naval equipment he could drag ashore from his ships. He also planned the demolition of military installations in the port area and elsewhere, and the destruction of the water and electric-power systems. Apparently, however, he did not plan all the wanton demolitions that took place. His orders were carried out by half-trained sailors who knew that their only future was death in battle. As a result of their carelessness, several major fires broke out in the city before the Americans arrived. Manila was a sprawling city, half old Spanish and half modern American. Near the mouth of the Pasig River, which flows through the center of town and empties into Manila Bay, was the old Spanish walled city of Intramuros. Its outer walls, constructed of great stone blocks, were fifteen feet thick, twenty-five feet high, and bordered on three sides by a moat. The struggle which developed in Manila fell into two parts—the fight for the city proper and the last desperate suicidal siege in the ancient citadel of Intramuros.

Iwabachi had no real plan for the defense of Manila except a fight to the death. However, he did decide to make his last stand in the walled city of Intramuros, and he prepared the most elaborate and ferocious defenses there. A semicircle of government buildings and schools, extending from the General Post Office to the river, was fortified with sandbags, and firing slits for machine guns were chopped through the outside walls. Tunnels from the basements of buildings led to outside pillboxes. All intersections were barricaded with barbed-wire entanglements, oil drums filled with sand or cement, and streetcar rails hammered upright into the roadway. Trucks and heavy factory machinery wrenched from buildings were set up as further obstacles in the streets. Mines of every type, including depth charges and airplane bombs, were placed in position to stop the American advance.

Iwabachi also mounted heavy naval 120-millimeter guns in buildings, dragged ashore some 200-millimeter naval rockets and even a few 450-millimeter giants; it was the first time in the Pacific war that the Japanese had used rockets. On the other hand, being a naval man, Iwabachi did not bother about snipers, who had played such a decisive part in other battles. It is doubtful that he would have got many even if he had wanted them, because most of his troops were either sailors or aircraft ground crews, and poor marksmen. Even so, these men, untrained and with no chance of escape, were to prove a very formidable enemy.

As their forward units encountered only light opposition in the outskirts of the city, the Americans had no warning of Iwabachi's intentions. General MacArthur shared Yamashita's military assessment of Manila and did not think he would have to fight for it. He had planned a great triumphal drive into the capital. This was hastily postponed as the Americans drove toward the center of town and encountered mines and streetcar tracks cemented into the roadway. Machine guns and heavy naval guns began to fire from every building. The post office, the city hall, the High Commissioner's residence, and the Manila Hotel were all heavily defended.

Yet Manila was never bombed. MacArthur would not permit it. General Walter Krueger, commander of the 6th Army, says in his book *Down Under to Nippon:*

> MacArthur told me personally he did not want the city proper, nor even Intramuros, to be bombed unless it was indispensably necessary. Nevertheless the physical damage was very great. Some districts were completely destroyed. The public buildings were badly wrecked and few buildings in the business section escaped total destruction.

The American Supreme Commander's order did not include a ban on the heaviest artillery fire, and the battle developed into a murderous old-fashioned siege, with American 105-millimeter howitzers firing point-blank and the Japanese replying with their heavy naval guns.

With all his communications cut, Yamashita knew nothing of this bloody battle until it had been raging for ten days. As soon as he learned of it he sent Iwabachi a message saying: "Withdraw at once in accordance with our original plan."

He also ordered General Yokoyama to counterattack and help Iwabachi withdraw his men. Upon receiving the message, the naval commander left the battle area to consult with Yokoyama, and it seemed as though he would obey Yamashita's orders. But he gave Yokoyama very little information about the situation in the city, and without waiting to learn the details of the counterattack, returned to Manila.

Iwabachi had left an Army officer, Colonel Noguchi, in command of the troops in the city. The naval personnel refused to obey Noguchi's orders and requested that a senior officer of their own service be brought into Manila. Iwabachi was very pleased to receive this message. He decided he was himself the appropriate officer and rejoined his forces.

It was not until four days later that Yamashita heard this news in his Baguio headquarters. He again insisted that Yokoyama make a counterattack and rescue the Admiral's troops. Yokoyama did finally attack, with two columns of several thousand men, but he was halfhearted in his attempt to save a commander who did not want to be rescued. After a three-day battle, he was thrown back by the Americans without much difficulty.

Twice more, Iwabachi received orders from Yamashita to withdraw, but he answered with a flat refusal, saying that any move now would only cause the annihilation of his troops, while if he remained in the city, he could cause heavy losses to the Americans. Very soon afterward he was surrounded. Even then, General Yokoyama suggested that he withdraw by infiltrating small groups of his men through the American lines at night. This had proved a successful operation more than once in the Pacific war. There was no recorded answer to this message because all communications had now ceased between the Japanese forces in Manila and the outside world.

When the American encirclement of the city was complete, Iwabachi still had more than six thousand men with him. As his forces were compressed into an ever-decreasing space, the fighting became more savage.

The blazing city of Manila was now a bloody nightmare. The Americans used 155-millimeter guns at point-blank range to batter buildings containing Japanese sailors. Knowing they were trapped and doomed, the sailors fought with double ferocity, until the buildings collapsed, burying them.

The three-day struggle for the Manila Hotel exhibited a breakdown of all civilized standards; the Japanese behaved like half-crazed beasts. When American infantry entered the hotel lobby, machine-gun fire was showered on them from the stairways and landings. The Japanese made repeated suicidal counterattacks from one floor to the next. Toward the end, the battle was fought chiefly in hand-to-hand encounters on rooftops. The Americans climbed onto the roofs and poured blazing gasoline and oil down through the air vents. Then the Japanese fought their way back to the top of the building and lobbed down hand grenades.

With the Japanese sailors were dozens of Filipino girls who had been dragged into the hotel before the battle. While the fighting was at its height, these unfortunate women were repeatedly raped. The sex orgies, followed usually by murders, continued until the hotel was finally surrendered. The atrocities spread all over the city. Many Japanese sailors, thinking they were soon to die and could never be punished, raped every Filipino woman they could seize during these days.

One girl was told by a Japanese sailor, who pointed across the Pasig River: "Although you cannot see them, the Americans are just over there and will soon be in this hotel. By that time, nothing will matter, because we will both be dead."

The sailor was correct in the prediction of his own fate: there were no Japanese survivors of the Battle of Manila.

The Americans began preparations for a final attack on the port area and the walled city of Intramuros, and opened up the greatest concentration of fire ever seen in the Pacific. Nine battalions of howitzers, with tank destroyers, tanks, and 4.2 mortars, battered the ancient citadel, smashing great holes in the walls. The Japanese answered with their naval guns, which had been hauled inside. Inside the fortress, the Japanese had built a series of tunnels so they could move troops and guns from one side to another very rapidly. The Americans realized that they had to attack in more than one place at a time to overwhelm this type of defense.

Before Intramuros fell, it was to be transformed into one of the worst scenes of devastation and death seen in World War II. Both sides, Japanese and American, in their different ways, behaved with the utmost savagery.

General Krueger, the attacking commander, blames most of the devastation on the demolition work of the Japanese. "By the places they set on fire there can be no doubt who was responsible." But he goes on to say: "Much of the destruction was caused by our own artillery fire. It could have been avoided if the Japanese, when further resistance on their part was clearly futile, had heeded several radio broadcasts urging them to surrender." The Americans fired 10,000 shells an hour into Intramuros, many of them from their heaviest howitzers.

The defenders had no intention of surrendering. In the burning citadel, rocked every second with heavy explosions, the Japanese were not only fighting like demons but also inflicting further horrors upon the unhappy Filipinos trapped there with them.

Drunken, bearded, bayonet-carrying Japanese chased doctors and nurses around the hospital. In Fort Santiago prison, gasoline was poured throughout the building and set alight, killing five thousand Filipinos in one cell block. When some of the frantic prisoners broke out of the building, they were machine-gunned. More than one hundred Filipinos were beheaded, one by one, over a three-hour period in the prison yard.

Five thousand women and children took refuge in Manila Cathedral. Many women were raped inside the building. When some, pleading for mercy, held up their babies, the soldiers impaled the children on bamboo spikes or bayonets and violated the mothers.

It was dusk when the Americans finally fought their way into the center of Intramuros, stumbling over heaps of carelessly piled corpses covered with fine gray ash and dust. Most of them had been killed by bayonet wounds or sword cuts. In the dungeons of Fort Santiago hundreds of Filipinos lay dead. The bodies of twenty-five men and women were found in the Church of Santo Domingo. Outside another church there were forty-five bodies in clerical robes, with their hands tied behind their backs; some had been shot, and others bayoneted.

The American 37th Infantry Division commander, Major General Robert S. Beightler, ordered his troops to take no more prisoners. This order was apparently based on three factors: (1) the Japanese refusal to obey the American demand for the surrender of Manila; (2) the savage fighting of the Japanese as the American Army approached Intramuros; and (3) the discovery of the atrocities perpetrated on the Filipinos.

Trying to obey their commander's orders, the American forces were considerably embarrassed in the heat of the battle when twenty Formosan labor troops suddenly gave themselves up. Not wanting to shoot them in cold blood, they sent a message back to General Beightler, whose reply was: "If you are unfortunate enough to take prisoners, they must be dealt with in the ordinary way."

All that night, fighting went on in the caves, dugouts, and tunnels of Intramuros. The next day, the battle continued in the dungeons of the ancient fortress. It was not until the end of the third day that the last defenders were annihilated.

The only organized resistance left in Manila was centered in three government buildings, built of reinforced concrete, with sandbag strong points and machine guns at every corner. The fighting at these was just as savage as in the previous battles. After their artillery had smashed through the walls, the Americans had to fight their way step by step up the stairways and then from room to room.

Eight days after the fall of Intramuros, the last Japanese force in Manila consisted of a small group of thirty men, holding out on the top of the elevator shaft in the Finance Building. Burning gasoline and grenades finally sent them to a fiery death down the shaft.

That was the end of the battle. Somewhere in the twisted, scorched ruins of Intramuros lay the charred, unidentifiable body of Admiral Iwabachi. It was never found. The battle had cost the lives of 16,000 Japanese. The Americans had lost 1,000 killed, and 4,600 wounded.

MacArthur's triumphal march into Manila never took place. No one could count the Filipino dead, and very little of the city was left standing.

CHAPTER 11

End on Prog Mountain

While the Americans were still fighting their way yard by yard into the smoking ruins of Manila, MacArthur was grouping his forces to strike against Yamashita's mountain stronghold. It became clear to the Americans, as they began to climb into the mountains, that the Japanese commander was going to defend not only the road to Baguio but every other approach as well.

Yamashita was determined to hold on as long as possible to the two-hundred-mile-long Cagayan valley, his only source of food. Getting supplies out of the valley was not an easy task. The roads were not wide enough and he was short of vehicles. Those he had were running on charcoal or pine oil, and they crept along very slowly and cautiously under constant American air attack.

Two months after the American invasion of Luzon, the Japanese troops were getting less than half a pound of rice a day instead of their minimum ration of two and a half pounds. A few weeks later, they were down to a spoonful a day. The number of deaths from tropical fevers like malaria, and beriberi and other diet-deficiency diseases, became greater than the number of those killed in combat.

In spite of this, the Americans did not make much headway. Yamashita had told his staff he was prepared to sacrifice a whole division to protect the rice in the Cagayan valley.

However, the position in Baguio, which was increasingly bombed, became so bad that he decided to withdraw farther into the mountains and make his headquarters at the small village of Bambang. This meant the abandonment of the valley, but he knew he could not hold it much longer. His decision was based on sound military principles. He had had almost three months in which to strip the Cagayan and neighboring valleys of food and other supplies. In this time, he had gathered nearly all the rice harvest and a new crop was not due before September. He did not have the strength to hold on until then.

His other motive for holding the valley had been to stop the Americans from using the airfields there, which could have provided a base for bombing attacks on Formosa and Okinawa. Also, he had wanted to keep the airfields in the hope that reinforcements and supplies might yet reach Luzon. Now that all prospect of reinforcement had gone, he felt that there was no longer any purpose in sacrificing men to hold the position.

One division was left to cover the last troop convoys as they climbed into the mountains. It had orders to withdraw once all the rice and food—including water buffaloes on the hoof—had been transported into the hills. He also left a strong rear guard in Baguio, with instructions to hold out as long as it could. Every able-bodied soldier in Baguio was sent forward for a last stand on the river gorge. They held up the Americans for five days, covering Yamashita's retreat and allowing him to evacuate 10,000 troops from the city.

Thousands of civilians from Baguio, mostly women and children, began to tramp up into the mountains to avoid the coming battle. Many of them died on the jungle tracks.

The day before he moved out, Yamashita called in the reporters and shared his last bottle of rice wine with them. He left at ten o'clock at night, his convoy looking more like a gypsy caravan than the headquarters of a commander in chief. Most of the supplies were carried by coolies or water buffaloes; soldiers carried as much as they could on their own backs. Yamashita traveled in a pine-oil-fueled car along a steep track which had been made just wide enough for vehicles. The night was overcast and starless. Vehicles, driving without lights, ran into one another on the dark road or slid over the hillsides. It took two hours to travel six miles. The next day, he was still only sixteen miles from Baguio.

He could hear the bombardment below as the Americans tried to force their way over the river into the hill town. Moving in the daytime was dangerous, so he hid under a tree and slept.

In the evening, the convoy started climbing very slowly in a jungle full of singing insects. At midnight on the second day, the road came to an end and all transport had to be abandoned. Yamashita continued his journey through the mango-tree jungle on horseback and later on foot. He and Muto used golf clubs, inherited from his playboy predecessor, as walking sticks.

The village of Bambang consisted of a few huts, thatched with leaves. Yamashita took over a small house by a mango tree near a shallow river. It was only six feet square but it seemed like a palace after the damp, dark cave at Baguio.

Everyone felt stronger and more confident in the clear mountain air. Yamashita discussed his plans with Muto and said that if he could hold up the American tanks until the start of the rainy season at the end of April, it would give him a chance to reorganize.

Meanwhile, his units were forced to destroy their tanks as they withdrew into the mountains. Most of the crews had brought their tanks from Manchuria and every scratch had memories for them. Before they set fire to the vehicles, the soldiers stroked them as though they were horses, and said: "May your soul rest in peace." Then they put on the white headbands that signified their readiness for death, and climbed into the mountains to fight as infantry.

The rainy season came at last and forced the Americans to slow up their attack. Heavy rain clouds grounded bombers but there was little respite for the hungry Japanese troops. Tropical diseases were increasing rapidly and hospital supplies had nearly run out. Most of the sick men just lay down in the jungle to die.

After the fall of Baguio, the Americans brought up a new division. They began to set fire to the jungle with phosphorus bombs before advancing. Their progress was slow; they suffered heavy losses each time they attacked a Japanese position. Also, the blinding rain and perpetual damp in the sunless jungle began to take its toll. The battle became a struggle for survival for both armies. Leaves continually dripped moisture in the gray, damp, ghostly forests and everywhere there was the sickening smell of decaying vegetation and bodies. And when the men lay exhausted on the ground, leeches sucked their blood.

The Japanese troops crouched in tiny foxholes, eating nuts, sucking moss, and sipping the one cup of water that was their daily ration.

They were still alert and savage. Every knoll and hill was used as a machine-gun emplacement. Caves, either natural or dug out, hid heavy mortars and guns. Holding on tenaciously by day, at night they crept out to counterattack. Even their wounded threw grenades at the advancing Americans.

The U. S. forces advanced slowly but inexorably. A month after he arrived in Bambang, Yamashita was forced to move again, deeper into the Sierra Madre Mountains, to the isolated hill village of Kiangan.

It was not only in the Philippines that matters were going badly for the Japanese. Imperial Headquarters were making plans for their last stand in Japan itself. They ordered Yamashita's chief planning officer to return to help prepare defenses in the home islands. He flew out at midnight from a secret mountain airstrip, on the last plane to leave the Philippines for Japan. Muto sent a letter home, but Yamashita did not. In Baguio the latter had received a message from his wife telling him that the adoption formalities for his brother's son had been completed. It seemed to give him a final satisfaction to know that in spite of his own childlessness there was now someone to carry on his name, whatever happened. When he heard that the last plane was leaving, he said: "I won't write a letter. I have sent my last letter to Tokyo. My business in my homeland is all finished."

At the same time, he lost communication with the front, and confusion broke out among the troops.

Separated from one another, units began to retreat in disorder toward the mountains, some bringing women and children with them.

One Japanese officer said, "The rivers were flooded by the heavy rains and most of the bridges washed away. As the American tanks rolled along the road toward Bambang, a group of Filipino refugees, including women and children, were trapped by them. When the tanks reached a riverbank, some of the women seemed to go mad. They hammered on the tanks with their fists, and shrieked. Others drank poison or threw themselves into the water to drown."

Having no antitank guns by now, the Japanese built roadblocks to stop the Americans, who promptly brought up bulldozers which either smashed the blocks or cleared paths around.

Yamashita decided to withdraw into the inhospitable, almost unknown valley of the Asin River. The Americans, with their fresh division, were moving faster than he had anticipated and had taken several positions which he had expected to hold for several weeks. When he formed his new line to defend the approaches to the upper Asin valley, one of the fiercest final battles of the campaign began.

Japanese troops erected new defenses along the road at the Rayambugan Farm School, near a river swollen by the rains. Though the water was rising rapidly, it was not yet at flood stage, and the U. S. 32nd Division managed to repair the bridge.

As the Americans approached the school, the Japanese destroyed several tanks with their two remaining field guns. The U. S. troops withdrew to the riverbank. The next day, American planes bombed the Japanese positions and destroyed what remained of their food. Twenty-four hours later, the Japanese were surrounded, but they fought back fiercely, and most of them escaped during the night.

Nearly two hundred Japanese jumped an American column, destroying two tanks and doing a great deal of damage to ammunition trucks and other vehicles. But, in spite of heavy rifle, machine-gun, and mortar fire, the Americans overran the Rayambugan Farm School.

That was virtually the finish of the battle of Luzon. Ten days later—June 26, 1945—all Japanese resistance ended in the Cagayan valley. It was the strategic end of the campaign in the Philippines.

Although Yamashita was still in an excellent defensive position in the mountains, with sufficient ammunition to hold on for a very long time, all his other supplies were exhausted. There was no clothing and hardly any medical supplies, and he estimated that his food would be completely finished by mid-September. His troops were also short of salt, without the proper intake of which the human body becomes rapidly exhausted, and tried to make it from the Asin River without much success.

Hunger was making them desperate. Forward units reported that soldiers hiding in the jungle would kill anybody for his rations. Messengers, who had to hide in the jungle until nightfall to avoid American bombers, made their way very cautiously at night, keeping a sharp lookout for starving murderers among their own troops. A messenger from Yamashita to the forward troops gave this description of his journey.

There were many Japanese soldiers dead in the jungle, their swollen bodies and rotting faces covered with maggots and flies. All along the track, tents contained skeletons in ragged clothes. At nighttime, it seemed as if their spirits were crying out.

I tried to write down the names of the dead or tell wounded men where the nearest hospital unit was. After a time, I gave up, as there were too many and hardly any of them had enough strength to walk to the nearest first-aid post.

Every river had swollen corpses floating on the surface. I came to a guard post and they told me a friend of mine had just died there. I placed a cigarette in front of his grave and prayed for him.

When I reached headquarters, they told me it had transferred two miles away up a steep track. It was the longest journey of my life. It took me two hours to make those two miles, mostly crawling, and I arrived shivering and dizzy. I thought I had a very severe attack of malaria.

They gave me two sweet potatoes and a spoonful of rice. Then I sat in front of a warm fire and soon felt all right again. A doctor told me I was suffering from exhaustion due to starvation.

Yet as the American forces prepared to follow the Japanese deeper into the Sierra Madre Mountains, they still faced a task of terrifying magnitude. Yamashita had 65,000 troops, who could look forward only to a slow death by starvation or disease if they were not first killed by the Americans. But in this mountain jungle, with its fever-ridden climate, they could still fight a fierce delaying action.

That was what Yamashita decided to do when he made his last headquarters on Mount Prog. This peak was nearly 10,000 feet high, and the mountain tribes regarded it as holy. It was still the rainy season as he and his staff ascended

Mount Prog, but he could see most of Luzon spread out below him. He gazed thoughtfully for a few moments at the land he had lost, then climbed on.

He decided to pitch camp at a place where there were a few crude, deserted habitations that had been used by a native tribe, the Igorot. His staff dug trenches in case of air attack and built grass huts.

Yamashita sat outside his hut, with a fly whisk in his hand, reading battle reports. All told the same story of defeat, but his only comment was: "The cnemy attacks my stomach. I must hug him closer to me to strangle him."

He refused to take a bath, because his soldiers could not do so, and only wiped his body with a dry towel. Food was now so short that a spoonful of rice was kept for special occasions. The troops subsisted on sweet potatoes and other wild vegetables.

To cheer up his officers, Yamashita distributed among them his last cigars. These were broken apart and smoked a few leaves at a time, wrapped in thin paper torn from the pages of an English-Japanese dictionary. He also served green tea in chipped china bowls he had brought from Baguio.

Many men were now so ill that although there was a river near the camp, most of them were too weak to try to catch fish or draw water from it. They drank muddy water out of the paddy fields and tried to snare snakes. Snake meat, which tasted like fishy chicken, had become a rare delicacy. One officer shot at a rat with the last round from his revolver. When he missed, he broke down and wept—he had lost his last chance to eat meat.

In the second week in July, the Japanese artillery fired their few remaining shells. After the last one was gone, they destroyed the guns, "like parents choking their own children," as one man described it.

At this time, General MacArthur broadcast that the battle for the Philippines was over, and that "only mopping up remained."

For weeks, communication had been severed between Yamashita and Terauchi's headquarters in Saigon. On July 30, however, a Morse radio channel reopened and Yamashita sent a code message to Southern Region Headquarters, stating that because of the food situation, all organized resistance must end early in September.

He told them that he had drawn up a plan in which, if he was attacked on Mount Prog, he would order his troops to escape to northwest Luzon, where they would find food and be able to fight on as guerrillas. He intended to command these guerrilla bands. Those who could not join him were to stage suicide attacks.

Yet, in spite of everything, the Japanese troops were still fighting in the rainy jungle, and the Americans could not force their way into the last stronghold in the Asin valley. In six weeks of fighting, the Japanese inflicted 16,000 casualties upon their enemy.

In the middle of August, as American mortar fire moved ever nearer the mountain, Yamashita and his staff ate a jungle chicken, the last real meal they had. Afterward the general, normally a stout man, pulled in three holes of his belt and tried to joke, saying: "I am getting very slim nowadays. I will be able to climb the mountains faster than you young boys." Those who listened to this remark noticed that his sunken eyes did not smile.

Then Tokyo broadcast a report that Soviet Russia had entered the war. When he heard this, Yamashita called a meeting of his staff officers, and said: "The land of our ancestors will be the last battlefield now. You must maintain military discipline and do your best to save the honor of the Japanese Army. All of you will soon have a chance to perform your last service to your country."

Events were moving very quickly outside his lonely, unmapped stronghold. He received a message from the Navy, reporting on a monitored San Francisco broadcast that said the Japanese government was trying to make peace through the Swiss, as long as it did not touch problems of national character—meaning the Emperor.

The end could not be long delayed. A few hours later, the radio said the war had ended by the Emperor's order. Yamashita had still heard nothing official.

No one on Prog Mountain talked much about the surrender. Yamashita drafted an order to the scattered troops, hoping it would reach most of them: "Try to maintain discipline for the honor of the Imperial Army. Rescue all patients and civilians from the mountains and try to secure as much food as you can. My most important duty is to send you all back to your native land."

That evening Yamashita sat in his small grass hut, which

was lighted only by a pine-oil lamp, and stared at the ceiling in silence. Muto, who was convinced that his superior would commit hara-kiri, said to him: "Please let me stay in your hut tonight."

Yamashita replied: "Don't worry. I won't go alone to die. I have a great duty still to see all my troops go back to Japan. Please go away. I won't leave you all." Then he lay down on his bed and closed his eyes.

When Muto left the hut, he was still apprehensive about Yamashita's intentions and said to the commander of the guard: "Watch the General carefully tonight." And he made a cutting gesture with his hand, indicating the ritual sword suicide. That night, while Yamashita slept, a senior staff officer maintained a vigil outside his hut, watching in case he tried to kill himself.

Next morning, he called his staff together and said: "I haven't had the Imperial order yet, but according to the radio, the surrender seems true. Now the situation has completely changed. All of you must fervently believe in the long life of Imperial Japan. You must not allow yourself to be shortsighted or moved by emotions. All of us must be careful to make no mistakes and to concentrate on the rebuilding of our country. In spite of what has happened, there are still many things to do, and I hope you will all do your best in these last moments of the war."

Many of the younger officers, differing from Muto, felt that Yamashita ought to kill himself to avoid the shame of imprisonment by the Americans. The following night, one of the officers who had been with him in Manchuria crept into the hut and begged him to choose an honorable death. "Please kill yourself, General," he begged. "I could not bear it if you were humiliated by our enemies."

Yamashita smiled. "I have killed many enemies and I am afraid some friends, too," he said. "I must pay for this. In my wildest dreams, I never believe I can return to Japan.

"But if I kill myself, someone else will have to take the blame instead of me. I must take this responsibility myself alone; that is why I have decided to live."

On August 19, an order came from Terauchi, saying: "Obey Imperial command. Fourteenth Army Group to cease fire and stop fighting. We forbid the Army to make treaty on the spot. Will dispatch staff officer as messenger. Let us know suitable airfield." This last order from Saigon showed that Southern Region Headquarters were, as usual, completely out of touch with the situation. Yamashita had not had control of an airfield for many weeks.

The younger officers became particularly curious about the phrase "Obey Imperial command." Did this mean that there was a body of opinion against the order? Did some people still wish to continue fighting? Also, the order contained no instructions about surrender. Yamashita, who would always obey his Emperor, began to worry that officers like the one who had pleaded with him to commit hara-kiri would refuse to submit, and continue the battle.

As days went by, he also became increasingly anxious about the shortage of food. Thousands of his troops were dying of starvation and disease every day while the High Command tried to send messengers to nonexistent airfields.

After a week, as he had still received no orders from Tokyo, he decided to act on his own initiative. He said: "If we are going to surrender, we must do it as early as possible and save the lives of soldiers who are dying of starvation and fever."

That day, a plane flew over Yamashita's headquarters and dropped a message from Major General W. H. Gill, of the American 32nd Division, stating that if he wanted to surrender he should send an envoy into the American lines. The following afternoon a Japanese captain, carrying a white flag, took a letter from Yamashita to Gill, offering to surrender. Yamashita pointed out, however, that he had not had any official confirmation of the Japanese capitulation. But he permitted an American radio group, escorted by a Japanese safe-conduct party, to climb the jungle paths to his Prog Mountain headquarters to take over communications and arrange details of the surrender.

Without waiting for any further instructions from Imperial Headquarters—which in fact did not come until five days later—he set off to walk into the American lines. He thought only of saving the lives of his starving soldiers and arranging their repatriation. His last order to his troops was: "I go to sign the cease-fire treaty in Baguio. You will disarm according to American orders."

On the morning of September 2, General Yamashita, thin but immaculate, walked down a jungle track into the American lines at Kiangan. His party was put into jeeps and driven to the government house in Baguio, where he handed over his samurai sword and signed the instrument of surrender.

Present at the meeting was one surprise visitor, General Percival, who had been flown by the Americans from his prison camp in Manchuria to attend Yamashita's official surrender. This is General Percival's account of what happened: "As General Yamashita entered the room where I was I saw one eyebrow lifted and a look of surprise crossed his face—but only for a moment. His face quickly resumed that sphinx-like mask common to all Japanese and he showed no further interest."

After he had signed the surrender in Baguio, Yamashita was told by the Americans that they proposed to hold him prisoner pending war-criminal charges against him. He was put under escort to be taken to the New Bilibid prison.

What had Yamashita achieved by his long battle in the mountains? He knew from the beginning that he did not have enough troops or supplies to prevent MacArthur from occupying the whole of Luzon. As early as December, 1944, he realized that his only chance was to hold up the Americans and stop their advance toward Japan, by pinning down as many of their troops as possible. Their air power and superior equipment made impracticable any counterattack he might mount. Instead, he decided to conserve his troops and establish strong defensive positions in the mountains, from which to conduct his long-drawn-out delaying actions. He withdrew to northern Luzon because the country there afforded him the best opportunity for a long-term defense and food was available in the Cagayan and neighboring valleys.

There is no doubt that his troops, under difficulties which he envisaged but which were much worse than anyone expected, did everything he asked of them. On August 15, the day of the Japanese surrender, Yamashita was still heavily engaging four reinforced American divisions.

The final balance sheet for the Battle of the Philippines was as follows: At the end of the campaign, Yamashita's forces were broken and incapable of offensive action. The principal strategic prize, the central plains–Manila Bay area, had been secured five months before. Nine of Japan's best divisions were destroyed and six others badly mauled. Japanese air power had been so battered that the desperate expedient of suicide pilots was employed for the defense of the homeland. When Japan lost control of the Philippines, her final defeat was only a matter of time.

However, the battle had been no walkover for the Americans. They had suffered 47,000 battle casualties, including more than 10,000 killed. The climate in Luzon, with its hot, dry days and cold, wet nights, had sent a further 87,000 American troops to the hospital.

The Japanese troops had proved themselves to be much more adaptable than had been expected. For instance, Yamashita's tank division, which withdrew into the mountains and left its vehicles behind, was rapidly retrained as infantry and held off the Americans for three months.

American intelligence was consistently ill informed and optimistic about the size of Yamashita's forces: they nearly always estimated his strength at half of what it really was.

When the war ended, there were over 100,000 Japanese still at large in the Philippines. More than 50,000 Japanese troops, who were still firmly under Yamashita's orders, came out of the mountains in northern Luzon, nearly 40,000 of them from the Asin valley. Thus the war in the Philippines ended with about one-third of the Japanese forces still alive and, if they could have obtained food, capable of conducting a fierce delaying operation.

The Americans have paid many grudging compliments to Yamashita's generalship and the fighting power of his troops. For instance, American Army historian Robert Ross Smith, who has written the official history *Triumph in the Philippines,* paid this tribute: "No one can ever dispute that Yamashita executed one of the most effective delaying actions in the whole history of warfare."

CHAPTER 12

The Trial

On October 29, 1945, two months after the Japanese surrendered to the Allies, General Tomoyuki Yamashita was tried in Manila as a war criminal. He was the first major enemy defendant to be placed in the dock, and on the opening day the courtroom had a grotesquely carnival air. The trial was held in the ballroom of the partly demolished United States High Commissioner's residence, facing the sunlit Manila Bay.

Arc lamps were anchored to the domed ceiling and movie cameramen and broadcasters jostled each other on the balconies. Outside, on Dewey Boulevard, six ice-cream vendors sold their product to the laughing Filipinos.

Wearing a green uniform, medals, and highly polished jackboots, Yamashita faced his accusers from the makeshift dock, his shaven head glistening under the bright lights. As they read out the indictment against him, his face revealed nothing.

There were 123 separate charges of crimes involving the deaths of 57,000 people. Most of the charges arose from the atrocities committed by the doomed, drunken, half-mad Japanese sailors in the nightmare battle for Manila. If any one man should have gone on trial for these horrors, it was their fanatical leader, Admiral Iwabachi. But his charred body lay somewhere under the ruins of the city he defended so ferociously.

Instead, Yamashita faced a military tribunal appointed by General MacArthur. Its president was Major General R. B. Reynolds, and four other generals acted as military judges.

The indictment accused Yamashita of "responsibility for brutal atrocities and other high crimes against the people of the United States and the allies and dependencies." The basis of the prosecution's case was that, while such high officers as Yamashita may not themselves have participated in atrocities, they must be held personally accountable. The fundamental theory behind the argument was that a commander must at all times be responsible for the actions of troops under his command. The prosecution split this into four points: (1) a commander should not carry out what is plainly an inhumane order; (2) Yamashita had command of all forces in the Philippines and therefore could have taken action on incidents involving naval forces; (3) the atrocities were so widespread and notorious that he could not have remained in ignorance of their existence except by taking positive steps not to be aware; and (4) while guerrillas may be summarily executed under the accepted laws of war, there is no civilized concept excusing torture.

The defense countered these accusations as follows: (1) the order for the extermination of the Filipinos and their property came to Yamashita from higher authority and he had no choice; (2) he was not in control of the naval troops which committed most of the Manila outrages; (3) he was unaware of the atrocities; and (4) the guerrillas had exhausted the patience of the Japanese.

The prosecution, fully aware that the trial hinged upon the question of the responsibility of a general for the acts of troops under his command, stated: "This will determine the precedent for future war-criminal prosecutions."

There seemed to be an undue haste in the setting up of the court, but General MacArthur had ordered his legal department to "proceed with the trial immediately." When the defense asked for more time to prepare their case, Colonel Alva Carpenter, chief of MacArthur's war-crimes section, said: "We will stand for no quibbling or unnecessary delay. This will be a military court and will follow strict rules of war. There will be no stalling."

Yamashita was fortunate, however, in the American officers who were chosen to defend him. After their first interview with him in his cell in the New Bilibid prison, near Manila, they became personally convinced of his innocence and fought his case right up to the United States Supreme Court and beyond to President Truman. They used every legal maneuver in their sustained battle to save his life, fighting for this enemy general with an ardor and determination far beyond the call of duty.

The hearing began with a number of sickening stories of Japanese atrocities. The defense at once pointed out that the majority of them had been committed by the Navy, over which Yamashita had no direct control, but the prosecutor, Robert M. Kerr, replied: "The atrocities were so notorious and flagrant that they must have been known to him." This set the note for the trial. There was to be no question of proving without reasonable doubt that the accused general knew about the atrocities; the prosecution set out merely to convince the court that "he must have known about them."

In the bitter postwar atmosphere, atrocities related by a sad and pitiable procession of survivors had a great influence on the court's attitude. According to the *New York Times*: "The court continued to hear stories of so many atrocities that people just sat dazed in their seats." Each story was worse than the last. The pitiful, often mutilated witnesses made such an impact on the tribunal that the generals sitting in judgment sometimes found their eyes wet with tears.

They heard a Chinese woman tell how her three-year-old son had been torn from her arms and bayoneted by a Japanese. After relating her story, she leaped suddenly from the witness stand and tried to claw at Yamashita as he sat in the dock. She was led sobbing from the court.

Then a seventeen-year-old girl, Julietta Milanes, described how her father and mother had been murdered during the siege of Manila. She turned to Yamashita and screamed: "If I could only get near you. You don't have shame. You ought to be hung. You ought to be cut in pieces. You can still laugh." Yamashita was certainly not laughing. Reporters noted that "his expression was one of puzzlement."

One of the most tragic witnesses was an eleven-year-old girl, Rosalinda Andoy, who told how her father was bayoneted to death and her mother killed by her side in a church in Intramuros where they had taken refuge. The Japanese then bayoneted her thirty-eight times. While speaking in

Tagalog, the native language of Luzon, she lifted her little pink frock to her neck to show the court the bayonet wounds. The generals on the bench wiped their eyes.

Apart from those committed in Manila, the prosecution held Yamashita responsible for two other major atrocities.

When the Americans landed, thousands of Filipinos in the wild Batangas province of Luzon joined the guerrilla movement. The court heard that as a reprisal 25,000 men, women, and children were brutally maltreated and killed in a deliberate attempt to exterminate much of the province. One survivor, Panfilo Umali, told the tribunal how three hundred men were forced to jump into a deep well. The Japanese threw stones after them and covered the opening with woven mats. He was one of seven survivors.

Three men who had escaped the massacre of the entire male population of four hundred in a village in Batangas province testified that after they and the others had been herded into an open space beneath a house, the Japanese blew up the building and fired the ruins with kerosene. Most of the survivors had been killed with hand grenades and bayonets.

The defense tried to bring out facts about the fierce guerrilla activity in Batangas province, but the prosecution objected to this, claiming that it was irrelevant. After twenty minutes of deliberation, the court sustained this objection but promised to admit " a limited amount" of testimony about guerrilla activity. The president, Major General Reynolds, emphasized that "the commission will not consider guerrilla activity as an excuse for cruelty."

Just as terrible an atrocity—and much more difficult to counter—was the infamous massacre at Palawan Island, where 151 American prisoners of war had been working as construction laborers on the airfield. When an American plane was seen overhead, the Japanese commander ordered all the prisoners into air-raid shelters, poured gasoline into the shelters and ignited it. Most of the trapped Americans were burned to death and those who managed to dash into the open were machine-gunned. Only nine men survived the massacre by climbing over rocks and swimming five miles to another island.

Defense counsel A. Frank Reel wrote in *The Case of General Yamashita:*

No eyewitnesses of this atrocity, either Japanese or American, were produced at the trial. It appeared to be due to the unreasoning and fanatical fear of the Japanese garrison commander. He thought the presence of an American aircraft might mean a landing on Palawan was imminent. He also heard a rumor that a powerful American convoy was approaching the island. His small company of Japanese barely outnumbered the prisoners and it was evident that he ordered the massacre because his tortured brain saw it as a defensive move.

There were no links between Yamashita and the Palawan atrocities. The Japanese soldiers who committed this deed were Air Force men. The massacre took place on December 14 and Yamashita was not given command of the Air Force until January 1, 1945—18 days later.

Reel added this rueful comment:

These were not Filipinos who had been slaughtered but American soldiers, sons and husbands of grief-stricken citizens of Ohio, Indiana, California and New York. The Japanese had done this deed and now vengeance was ours.

The prosecution's case boiled down to the fact that Yamashita should have done something about the matter, regardless of whether he had the right or power to do it. This was the most bloody of crimes. The accused must answer for it—simply because he was the accused. There must be revenge.

The prosecution attempted to prove that all these atrocities had either been planned or agreed to by Yamashita. Their star witness was a fifty-nine-year-old Filipino political writer named Narciso Lapuz. The court president described his evidence as "testimony from behind the lines." Lapuz had had a varied and mysterious career. When the Japanese occupied Manila, he was condemned to death, then reprieved on condition that he serve General Artemio Ricarte, a rebel Filipino who had refused to accept American government of the Philippines and had once taken refuge in Japan.

The court listened in silence while Lapuz recounted how Ricarte had told him, upon Yamashita's arrival, that the general was "famous for his cruelty and responsible for many deaths." Shortly afterward, Ricarte, according to Lapuz, said: "This is terrible. Yamashita has issued a general order to wipe out the Filipino people, if possible. He regards us as enemies because we are either guerrillas or helping guerrillas."

Lapuz then went on to disclose an extraordinary military plan which, according to him, Yamashita had revealed to Ricarte. The Japanese commander proposed to move all his troops and heavy guns into the mountains, to allow the Americans to enter Manila. Then, the moment the Americans came, the Japanese would return and not one Filipino would remain alive. Lapuz added: "Ricarte told me that Yamashita had issued orders to all his military commanders that when the Americans were about to land, if any Filipino showed pro-American actions, the whole population of cities, towns, and villages was to be wiped out."

He alleged that Ricarte pleaded with Yamashita to countermand these orders, but the "Tiger of Malaya" refused, saying that he had received instructions for the massacre from the Japanese High Command. After the third meeting, Ricarte returned sadly and said to Lapuz: "This man has no heart."

Yamashita's counsel frequently interrupted Lapuz' evidence on the ground that it was all hearsay. The court, however, overruled all his objections. When the defense questioned him, Lapuz admitted that he was one of the first persons to be arrested by the Americans as a collaborationist and was in fact still in prison. He decided to produce his information only after his arrest. The chief defense counsel, Colonel Harry E. Clarke, of Arizona, said that Lapuz not only was anti-American but had been very active in the black market during the Japanese rule. When Clarke cross-examined him, Lapuz admitted that no one trusted him and even the Japanese had kept him under constant surveillance during their occupation of the Philippines. When this remark was interpreted to Yamashita, he sat back and laughed for the first time.

Lapuz also claimed to have freed 10,000 Filipinos from Fort Santiago. American counterintelligence investigators testified that their information was that he had probably freed a few—for a price. They also said that Lapuz had written to the chief of counterintelligence, offering a complete exposure of Japanese activities in the Philippines. In return for this information, he requested immunity and free transport to New York for himself, his family, and his servant. Under cross-examination, Lapuz denied he had ever written such a letter.

General Ricarte, an old man, had died at the time of the surrender. Lapuz admitted that no one else was present when Ricarte had made the alleged statements about Yamashita. Colonel Clarke asked: "Then all your testimony is based on the word of a dead man?" Lapuz replied: "He wasn't dead when he told me these things."

Lapuz' story was backed up by another resident of the New Bilibid prison, his brother-in-law, Joaquin Galang, who said that in December, 1944, he went to tea at the home of General Ricarte when Yamashita was present. Ricarte's grandson, who had been brought up in Japan while the general was in exile, acted as interpreter. According to Galang, the child told him that Yamashita said: "All Filipinos are guerrillas, even those who are supposed to be on General Ricarte's side."

Ricarte asked his grandson to reply: "They are only guerrillas because the Japanese took their food and tortured them." Galang said that Yamashita huffily refused to discuss the matter any more, adding: "Filipinos are very treacherous and are our enemies."

Through his grandson Ricarte made one more attempt, saying: "I would like to take this opportunity to ask you to withdraw your order to kill all Filipinos and destroy our city of Manila." Galang alleged that Yamashita stood up very angrily and shouted: "This is my order and it will not be disobeyed."

After their evidence was completed, American counter-intelligence agents produced records revealing that both Galang and Lapuz had been active Japanese agents and had presumably made up their stories to save their skins.

The defense called Ricarte's grandson, a fourteen-year-old named Biscumino Romero. When questioned about Galang's story of the tea party, he told the court in a clear, youthful voice: "I never once saw General Yamashita at my grandfather's house. They never talked together. If they did, I never at any time acted as interpreter for them."

The prosecution, in their opening address, promised to show films which would prove Yamashita's guilt beyond question. The film turned out to be a propaganda movie made in Hollywood before the war ended. It was called *Orders from Tokyo,* and purported to show the destruction of Manila and the death and maiming of the Filipinos trapped in Intramuros. Its most dramatic scene showed an American soldier bending over the body of a dead Japanese. He reached into the corpse's pocket and slowly took out a piece of paper. As he did so, the commentator intoned in a grave voice: "Orders from Tokyo. We have discovered secret orders to destroy Manila." The voice added "This is evidence which will surely convict Yamashita."

Defense counsel Reel wrote in *The Case of General Yamashita:*

> No explanation of how the American soldier was able to read Japanese or what an ordinary Japanese infantryman was doing with a top-secret high-command order in his pocket was ever given to the court. Not that it was not asked for. The defense pleaded with the prosecution to produce the order. They never did.

The head of the Allied translation service, Captain Norman Sparnom of the Australian Army, testified that hundreds of thousands of Japanese military documents had been captured, many of them mimeographed orders. Not one could be found that ordered the destruction of Manila, the killing of noncombatant civilians, or the execution of prisoners of war. The captain stated: "If there was such an order, it would have been given immediate priority because it was of such high intelligence value."

As the trial proceeded, the type of evidence produced by the prosecution and allowed by the court began to have a disquieting effect on many observers, including British and American newspaper correspondents. After the court had been sitting for two weeks, Robert Trumbull, of the *New York Times,* sent this dispatch:

> The trial of General Yamashita marks the first time a military man has ever been brought before the bar of justice to answer for atrocities committed by his troops in war. Interest among students of international law, and of American military law, is most intense for the Board hearing the Yamashita case is setting precedents for all time.
>
> All precedents in law have been thrown out the win-

dow in the Yamashita case because this itself is without precedent. There are no regulations governing the American War Crimes Commission, except those it makes for itself, and it has made very few.

War criminal trials in the Philippines so far are entirely in MacArthur's hands. General MacArthur wanted no assistance—or would he call it meddling?—by the War Department Commission trying the Nazis. That point decided, it was apparent to him that the Articles of War do not apply to the Japs, for they are not members of the U. S. Armed Forces. Rules governing courts-martial are out—this is not a court-martial.

So on Sept. 24, 1945—40 days after the Japanese surrender—there came from General MacArthur's Tokyo H.Q. a directive entitled "Rules Governing the Trial of War Criminals." This six page document contains 22 brief, simply phrased regulations which are the only rules governing the conduct of these trials.

The defendant's rights are to make his case before the judges, who are told they must be impartial. He must have a copy of the charges and specifications before the trial. He may have counsel of his own choice who may present relevant evidence, call witnesses on his behalf, cross-examine adverse witnesses. And he may have the proceedings translated to him if he cannot understand them.

The rules of evidence set forth in MacArthur's directive boil down to: anything goes.

Hearsay can be admitted, and has been. Any sort of documents—affidavits, depositions, even letters and diaries—are admissible although such procedure abridges the defense's right of cross-examination.

Newsweek magazine reported that spectators were "scandalized by the break with Anglo-Saxon justice," adding: ". . . even third hand hearsay is admitted as evidence. . . . In the opinion of probably every correspondent covering the trial, the military commission came into the courtroom the first day with the decision clearly in its collective pocket."

Henry Keyes sent this dispatch to his newspaper, the London *Daily Express:*

Yamashita's trial continued today—but it isn't a trial. I

doubt if it is even a hearing. Yesterday his name was mentioned once. Today it was not brought up at all.

The Military Commission sitting in judgment continued to act as if it were not bound by any law or rules of evidence. I have no brief for any Japanese but in no British court of law would the accused have received such rough and ready treatment as Yamashita.

The Yamashita trial has been hailed as the most important in the Pacific not because it is the first but because the present Commission is supposed to be setting precedents for all future war criminal trials. The trial is supposed to establish that a military commander is responsible for any acts of any of his troops. At the same time, under British law anyway, he is supposed to have rights.

The present Commission pleads saving time and money but the facts so far are Yamashita's American counsel have not had a hearing. Under the laws of the U. S. Congress, affidavits in criminal cases are inadmissible. Yet one question and answer in one affidavit was described by the defense as not only double hearsay but hearsay based on conjecture. It was extremely prejudicial, put in for prejudicial reasons by the prosecution.

A long line of high-ranking Japanese officers testified on behalf of Yamashita but, since many of them were themselves about to be tried as war criminals, their evidence did not make much impression on the court. One of the most important of them was an elderly man, looking like a farmer, in a creased, patched uniform and dirty cracked boots. He was Vice Admiral Okochi, the former commander of the Japanese naval forces in the Southwest Pacific. Giving his evidence in crisp tones, he stated: "Yamashita had tactical command over the 15,000 naval troops who were involved in the Manila affair but I, not Yamashita, had disciplinary powers over them." He added: "Yamashita ordered the evacuation of Manila but it could not be carried out because the transport was damaged. It was I, not Yamashita who ordered the destruction of Manila harbor and the other naval installations."

The former chief of the Japanese General Staff and commander of the Kwantung Army, General Umezu, also gave evidence. He said that no order had ever been issued in the

Japanese Army for the massacre of civilians or the mistreatment of prisoners, and stated: "If such an order had been issued, it would certainly have come to my notice."

Another witness was Lieutenant General Yokoyama, who had commanded the rear guard left by Yamashita outside Manila. He asserted: "It was Iwabachi who was in charge of the 16,000 naval troops who perpetrated the Manila atrocities. At this time, Yamashita was 150 miles away in Baguio. Yamashita's orders, which I relayed to Iwabachi, told him to be fair in all dealings with Filipino citizens and that there was to be no street fighting in the city. On the contrary, he ordered him to prepare a defense line outside the city."

Among the lesser officers who gave evidence was Colonel Hiroshi Hashimoto, chief of staff of the Manila defenses, who said that 1,800 Army troops had been left in the city to guard supplies and bridges, and 15,000 to 20,000 naval troops were also there. He picked out on a map the Navy positions, showing that the atrocities had been worst there.

Major General Goichi Kira, commander of the supply services on Luzon, who had been responsible for feeding 250,000 troops, prisoners, and internees, said that Yamashita always insisted that the internees receive a food supply equivalent to the Army's.

Lieutenant Colonel Kikuo Ishikawa, a transport and supply officer, said that when he surrendered, he had in his pocket a copy of a Tokyo order to treat prisoners in a friendly manner, and when the Americans approached, to leave as much food and medicine with them as possible. To this Yamashita added his personal warning not to ill-treat prisoners or internees when the Japanese withdrew, Ishikawa alleged that the document was taken from him when he surrendered.

Yamashita's former chief of staff, General Muto, became so indignant in his evidence that he was reprimanded by the tribunal. He said: "It is a piece of low comedy to suggest, on the evidence of one or two Filipinos, that Yamashita ordered a massacre. The idea, of course, is to publish to the world that the Japanese officers and soldiers are brutal and uncivilized—and so are the people of Japan. Yamashita is brought before the court as a victim for that reason."

A month after the trial began Yamashita took the witness stand to give evidence in his own defense. This is how the *New York Times* reported the scene:

In a 45 minute dramatic oration, the simple eloquence of which shone even through an interpreter's version, Yamashita disclaimed responsibility for the atrocities committed by his troops in the Philippines. With his large shaven head thrust forward and his eyes narrowed to brown slits under the floodlights, the Tiger of Malaya vowed to punish his subordinates who committed atrocities "to the fullest extent of the military law if circumstances permit."

The prosecution's first question to Yamashita was: "If you did not want to fight in Manila, why did you not make it an open city?" Yamashita replied:

It is recognized by international law that if a city is declared an open city, all defense equipment and military supplies should be taken away. I had neither the transport, the fuel, nor the time to carry all my supplies out of the city. Manila had been used as a main base for three years and many supplies and war materials had piled up there. It was also the Navy's main base and I had no authority over the Navy. They did not agree it should be an open city to protect it from American bombardment. In view of this, I could not break the rules of war. So I did the next best thing, which was to remove my army out of the city and try to keep it out of the battlefield.

On the question of the atrocities in Manila, he said: "In February, 1945, much brutality arose in those days of bloody incidents. I cannot tell you about the Japanese participants in these acts because they are all dead now. Those bloody incidents which arose were utterly against my orders."

Asked about the "Orders from Tokyo," which were alleged to have included a plan to wipe out all the inhabitants of Manila, he replied: "I had about 100,000 men on Luzon to resist the United States forces. Even if they had not been fully engaged, it would have been impossible for them to have murdered a million people, even if I had wished it."

He firmly denied that he ordered the destruction of buildings and other property in Manila: "I never issued such an order, but I did order the destruction of militarily important bridges. I had no knowledge of the construction of pillboxes and other defenses in Manila because my orders were that the city was to be evacuated."

He added that his policy toward prisoners of war was that "they should be treated exactly as officers and men of the Japanese forces are treated."

Questioned about the Palawan incident, his answer was that the garrison was under the orders of the 4th Air Force at that time and he had no jurisdiction over it.

He admitted his responsibility to protect civilians against unlawful acts by Japanese soldiers, ". . . if the Japanese forces did these acts and if I knew about them. As it was, I was absorbed with military operations."

The prosecutor, Major Robert N. Kerr, leaned forward and asked: "Is it a recognized duty among soldiers for a commanding officer to command his troops so they do not commit wrongful acts?"

Yamashita replied: "It is a recognized duty."

Then the following dialogue took place between the American military prosecutor and the accused Japanese general:

"Is it a wrongful act for a soldier to commit rape?"

"Not only for a soldier is that a wrongful act."

"Is it a wrongful act for a soldier to kill unarmed civilians without trial?"

"Yes."

"Is it a wrongful act for soldiers to torture people?"

"It is a prohibited act."

The prosecutor then said slowly: "I ask you to look at this map representing the Philippines. Each red pin represents a major violation of the laws of war which, according to the testimony in this case, was committed by your troops. According to this evidence, approximately 60,000 unarmed men, women, and children were killed in the Philippines by men under your command. Do you deny to the commission that you ever knew or heard of these killings?"

Yamashita: "I never heard of them nor did I know of these events."

Major Kerr: "This is your opportunity to explain to the commission, if you wish to do so, how you could have failed to know of these killings."

Yamashita paused, screwed up his eyes under the glaring lights, and took the opportunity offered. In clear, slowly articulated Japanese syllables, he began a short speech in his defense:

The facts are these: I was under constant attack by large American forces, which meant I was under pressure night and day to plan, study, and carry out plans to combat superior American forces. That took all my time and effort.

At the time of my arrival in the Philippines, I was not familiar with the situation. Nine days after my arrival, I was confronted with a superior American force about to land on Leyte. I did not have time to make a personal inspection and coordinate units under my command.

The source of true coordination of a command lies in trusting your subordinate commanders. I was forced to confront superior U. S. forces with subordinates whom I did not know and with whose character and ability I was unfamiliar. As a result of the inefficiency of the Japanese Army system, it was impossible to unify my command, and my duties were extremely complicated. The troops were scattered and Japanese communications were very poor.

When the Americans landed at Leyte, Mindoro, and Luzon, our communications were completely disrupted. Although we managed to maintain some liaison, I gradually became cut off and found myself completely out of touch with the situation. I believe that under these conditions I did the best possible job I could have done.

My plans and strength were not adequate to the situation, and if these atrocities happened, they were absolutely unavoidable and beyond anything I could have anticipated. If I could have foreseen these things, I would have concentrated all my efforts toward preventing them.

He paused for a moment, looked around the completely silent courtroom, and continued:

Certain testimony has been given that I ordered the massacre of all Filipinos. I wish to state that I did not order this. I did not receive such orders from higher authority nor did I permit such a thing. I will swear to heaven and earth as to the truth of all these points. That is all I have to say.

Major Kerr asked one more question. "You admit, do you, that you failed to control your troops in the Philippines?"

Yamashita paused, then answered loudly, with intense conviction:

> I have put forth my maximum effort in order to control my troops. If this was not sufficient, then somehow I should have done more. Some people may have been able to do more. I feel I did my best.

Then he sat down. It was his last word. The rest was up to his team of American defense lawyers. They had not been idle. Apart from cross-examining prosecution witnesses and calling a large number of people to testify for the defense, they had explored every legitimate method to save his life. Captain Reel put the situation like this:

> On the question of his responsibility for the rapes in the two Manila hotels, I find it difficult to see how anyone could believe that General Yamashita would order his men to commit rape or that he would condone such deeds if he found out about them. Not only is there no military advantage to be gained from rape but it is the sort of thing every commander fears and abhors because of its disastrous effect on the morale of his men.

Another defense counsel, Lieutenant Colonel Walter Hendrix, of Atlanta, Georgia, was even more vehement. He was convinced that Yamashita was being railroaded and alleged that the mood of General MacArthur was such that "the defense has been told that if Yamashita were sentenced to death today, he would be dead in forty-eight hours." He described the MacArthur regulations governing the war-crimes trials as founded on "a theory of no law at all" and also stated that MacArthur had instructed Lieutenant General Wilhelm D. Styer, Army commander in the Western Pacific, not to spend more than twenty-four hours reviewing Yamashita's case at the end of the trial.

The defense filed a plea of habeas corpus in the Philippine Supreme Court on these grounds: (1) charges against Yamashita did not state violations of the law of war; (2) the military commission had no jurisdiction in the Philippines, where there were no martial laws, no military government, and no hostilities; and (3) the rules did not afford fair trial in that they violated acts of Congress and the Articles of War as well as the United States and Philippine Constitutions. On the day that Yamashita took the stand in his own defense, the Philippine Supreme Court informed his lawyers that it lacked jurisdiction. It also decided that MacArthur's military tribunal had been "validly constituted."

As the case neared its end, the *New York Times* assessed the closing speech of the chief prosecutor, Major Kerr:

> Since no testimony and no documents were produced to link Yamashita beyond all reasonable doubt with complicity in the atrocities, the chief prosecutor chose to liken the case to manslaughter as a result of criminal negligence or alternatively "disinterest in the welfare of prisoners of war, internees and the Filipino population."
>
> The trial was conducted entirely under the brief rules drawn up by General MacArthur's legal staff and set precedents for the trial of war criminals which were watched throughout the world. The verdict on Yamashita's culpability will be a precedent in such similar cases as may arise from now on throughout all history.

The trial lasted thirty-two days. A tropical afternoon sun shone through the window of the Manila courtroom when the five generals of the military tribunal filed in to announce their verdict. Yamashita stood expressionless while the president, General Reynolds, said: "According to a secret ballot with a written vote of two-thirds or more members concurring, we find you guilty as charged. You are sentenced to death by hanging."

When the verdict was translated to him, Yamashita wrote in his notebook: "The truth can move the heavens." He was about to sign it "Great Cedar," but crossed out the characters before handing it to his interpreter. Then, bowing slightly to the judges, he walked out of the dock. Everyone in court silently watched his retreating back.

By what the newspapers described as "a strange coincidence," his death sentence was pronounced on December 7, 1945, the anniversary of the Japanese attack on Pearl Harbor four years before.

That night, Yamashita had a final talk with Muto. He said: "Please ask the United States Army to allow our men to go home as soon as possible. This is my last order as your superior officer." Then he was divested of his uniform and all his decorations, given GI fatigues, and escorted to the condemned cell.

The defense had fully realized that there could be only one verdict, because of the manner in which evidence had been admitted and the way the tribunal was constituted, and therefore had already decided to take the matter to higher authority. Radiograms were flying between Washington and Manila, asking for permission to file a habeas corpus with the United States Supreme Court; they were followed by a long airmail document, drafted by the defense counsel and signed by Yamashita.

Faced with this, the Solicitor General, J. Howard McGrath, argued that Yamashita had no rights in the United States. He advanced a strange argument, insisting that although hostilities had ended it was still a time of war. The Supreme Court disagreed with him and decided to hear Yamashita's case. The Secretary of War sent a direct order to General MacArthur, telling him to fly the three defense lawyers to Washington. The message said: "The court desires to hear arguments upon the questions presented and wishes to see the defense lawyers so they may hear the benefit of their arguments."

After the Supreme Court heard the defense's arguments, "In the Matter of the Application of General Tomoyuki Yamashita," the jurists—Chief Justice Stone and Justices Black, Frankfurter, Douglas, Murphy, Rutledge, and Burton —reserved their judgment. Then, after nearly a month's consideration, they dismissed the appeal. Giving judgment, Chief Justice Stone said:

> A commanding general must be held responsible for the conduct of his troops. . . . It is evident that the conduct of military operations by troops, whose excesses are unrestrained by orders or efforts of their commander, would most certainly result in violations which it is the purpose of the law to prevent. Its purpose to protect civilian populations and prisoners of war from brutality would largely be defeated if the commander of an invading army could with impunity neglect to take reasonable measures for their protection.

At the end of his judgment, Chief Justice Stone went out of his way to compliment Yamashita's defense counsel, stating: "This high concept of military justice is one of the basic protections of our system."

The court, however, was not unanimous; Justices Rutledge and Murphy dissented strongly. Their remarks on the case were an outstanding contribution to the ideals of American justice and have gone down into international legal history.

Justice Murphy was more qualified—though he also might have been more prejudiced—than anyone else in the matter, because he once had been Governor General of the Philippines. In his thirty-two-page dissenting judgment, with which Justice Rutledge concurred, he criticized the admission of improper evidence, including letters, reports, newspaper articles, and hearsay testimony, adding:

This trial is unprecedented in our history. Never before have we tried and convicted an enemy general for actions taken during hostilities or otherwise in the course of military operations or duty—much less have we condemned one for failing to take action.

The dissenting judgment continued:

This petitioner was rushed to trial under an improper charge, given insufficient time to prepare an adequate defense, deprived of the benefits of some of the most elementary rules of evidence, and summarily sentenced to be hanged. In all this needless and unseemly haste there was no serious attempt to prove that he committed a recognized violation of the laws of war.

He was not charged with personally participating in acts of atrocity or with ordering or condoning their commission. Not even knowledge of the crimes was attributed to him. It was simply alleged that he unlawfully disregarded and failed to discharge his duty as commander to control the operations of the members of his command, permitting them to commit acts of atrocity. The recorded annals of warfare and the established principles of international law form not the slightest precedent for such a charge.

This indictment, in effect, permitted the military commission to make the crime whatever it willed, dependent upon its biased view as to the petitioner's duties and his disregard thereof—a practice reminiscent of that pursued in certain less respected nations in recent years.

In our opinion such a procedure is unworthy of the traditions of our people or of the immense sacrifices they have made to advance the ideals of mankind. The high feelings of the moment will doubtless be satisfied but, in the sober afterglow, will come the realization of the boundless and dangerous implications of the procedure sanctioned today.

No one in a position of command in any army from sergeant to general can escape these implications. Indeed the fate of such future President of the United States and his Chiefs of Staff and military advisers may well have been sealed by this decision.

To subject an enemy belligerent to an unfair trial, to charge him with an unrecognized crime, or to vent on him our retributive emotions, only antagonizes the enemy nation and hinders the reconciliation necessary to a peaceful world.

The judge, drawing upon his knowledge of the troubled history of the Philippines, went on to comment:

That there were brutal atrocities inflicted upon the helpless Filipino people, to whom tyranny is no stranger, is undeniable. That just punishment should be meted out to all those responsible is also beyond dispute. But these factors do not justify the abandonment of our devotion to justice in dealing with a fallen enemy commander. To conclude otherwise is to admit that the enemy has not only lost the battle but has destroyed our ideals.

Justice Murphy concluded gravely:

Today the life of General Yamashita, a leader of enemy forces vanquished in the field of battle, is to be taken without regard to the due process of law. There will be few to protest. But tomorrow the precedent here established can be turned against others.

A procession of judicial lynchings without due process of law may now follow. No one can foresee the end of

this failure of objective thinking and adherence to our
high hopes of a new world. The time for effective vigi-
lance and protest, however, is when the abandonment of
legal procedure is first attempted. A nation must not
perish because in its natural frenzy of the aftermath of
war it abandoned its central theme of the dignity of
the human personality and due process of law.

The dissenting judges finished their remarks at three-thirty
in the afternoon. Within a few minutes, General MacArthur
was notified by radio that the Supreme Court had refused to
issue a writ of habeas corpus in the case of General Yamashita. Photostatic copies of the judgment were hastily prepared and flown to him in Tokyo. The triumphant victor of
the Philippines wasted no time in issuing this statement to
the press: "Yamashita will be hanged, stripped of uniform,
decorations, and other appurtenances signifying membership
of the military profession."

This was followed by one of those pieces of gothic prose
with which General MacArthur occasionally regaled the
world:

It is not easy for me to pass judgment upon a defeated
adversary in a major campaign. I have reviewed the
proceedings in a vain search for some mitigating circumstances on his behalf. I can find none.

Rarely has so cruel and wanton a record been spread
to the public gaze. Revolting as it may be in itself, it
pales before the sinister and far-reaching effects thereby
attached to the profession of arms. A soldier, be he friend
or foe, is charged with the protection of the weak and
unarmed. It is the very essence and reason for his being.
When he violates this sacred trust, he not only pro-
fanes his entire cult but he threatens the very fabric of
international society. The traditions of fighting men are
long and honorable, based upon the noblest of human
traits—sacrifice.

This officer of proven field merit, and entrusted with
high command involving authority adequate to his
responsibility, has failed his duty to his troops, to his
country, to his enemy and to mankind. He has failed
utterly his soldier's faith.

The transgressions resulting therefrom, as revealed

by the trial, are a blot upon the military profession and a stain upon civilization. They constitute a memory of shame and dishonor that never will be forgotten. Particularly callous and purposeless was the sack of the ancient city of Manila, with its Christian population and countless historic shrines and monuments of culture and civilization, which had previously been spared.

No new or retroactive principles of law, either national or international, are involved. The case is founded upon basic fundamentals and practice as immutable and as standardized as the most matured and irrefragable of social codes.

The proceedings were guided by that primary rationale of judicial purpose—to ascertain the full truth, unshackled by any artificialities of narrow views or technical arbitrariness. The results are beyond challenge.

There was only one more step open to the defense; they appealed for clemency to President Truman. Within a short time, a reply came from Washington: "The War Department has been advised that the President will take no action on the petition for clemency filed by counsel for General Tomoyuki Yamashita. General MacArthur has been given this information."

Yamashita had run out of chances. He was taken in great secrecy to a small local prison at Los Baños, outside Manila. MacArthur and his generals feared that the tens of thousands of Japanese prisoners of war now in their hands might riot when they heard of their general's fate. Extraordinary and clumsy precautions were taken. At midnight before the morning of execution, all Japanese prisoners were made to stand in the middle of their compounds, guarded by GI's with machines guns. This strange behavior on the part of their victorious enemy puzzled them, but soon it gave rise to a rumor that Yamashita was being hanged that night. As several of the Japanese who stood in the compound put it: "We were sorry for the General but we were too hungry, fed up, and war-weary to consider any form of protest. All we wanted to do was to go home."

The night before he was hanged, Yamashita ate some asparagus and bread and drank a can of American beer. Then he lay down and slept, snoring loudly.

At three o'clock in the morning, while the Japanese prisoners were still standing in the open under guard, he walked into the execution shed, attended by a white-robed Buddhist priest. An American military policeman who acted as his escort said afterward: "The attitude of the General was great. He stood on the steps of the gallows, faced toward the Imperial Palace, and seemed to be praying."

He bowed to the Buddhist priest, who was now sobbing loudly, and said clearly: "I pray for the Emperor's long life and prosperity forever." A few seconds later, the Oriental general who liked to be called Great Cedar, and whom others called the Tiger of Malaya, was dead.

The prisoners of war did not demonstrate against the execution, but a petition asking that Yamashita's life be spared was circulated among the civilian population in Japan, and 100,000 persons signed it on the first day. When the news of his hanging was published, there were demonstrations with placards on the Ginza, the main street of Tokyo. The Japanese press was forbidden to publish any comment on the execution, for under the censorship imposed by the Americans any unfavorable reaction to the Yamashita case would have been deemed criticism of the occupation rule. The foreign press, however, had no censorship restriction, and recorded the man in the street's opinion that "Yamashita was the scapegoat for an outmoded military system which it was not in his power to change."

The day after the hanging, Japanese officers imprisoned in the Philippines decided to gather near the wall of their camp for one minute at noon to pray for his soul. When they began to collect, they found that a group of Koreans and Formosans were standing there already, quietly praying for him. This was very unusual, because troops of these nationalities normally hated the Japanese officers under whom they served.

On that same day, there was a ghoulish footnote to his execution. Chinese and Filipino merchants came to the prison camp and offered for sale six-inch lengths of the rope which they claimed had been used to hang him. Nearly three thousand Japanese soldiers bought a piece of this rope. When they returned to Japan, scores of them called on the General's widow and reverently presented her with it.

Mrs. Yamashita's only official notification of her husband's fate was a note, reading: "Army General Yamashita Tomoyuki. This is to inform you that the above man was executed as a war criminal at Manila Luzon Island at 3:27 A.M. on the 23rd February 1946 according to the law and by order of army G.H.Q., U.S.A. in the Pacific Ocean."

Of Yamashita, General Muto wrote: "He was executed for the crimes which he knew nothing of, which his men committed regardless of what he said. Yamashita did his best, as a Japanese warrior should, and I believe our General is innocent. I can only depend upon the judgment that will be made by future historians." Muto was himself later hanged for complicity in the same war crimes.

Yamashita's Japanese biographer, Shuji Oki, has this to say about him:

People will say that Yamashita was a tragic general, an unfortunate general. Others will say there was no other general like him in the war in the Far East. He attained the highest honor as a warrior when he captured Singapore.

Yet if he had not been executed for Manila, he would surely have been executed by the British Army for his conquest of Singapore. If he had stayed in Manchuria, he would surely have been killed or captured by Soviet forces. Therefore, although he was hanged, the Philippines was the best place for him to die.

General Arthur Percival had no reason to like Yamashita, who defeated him at Singapore and caused him to be a prisoner of war in Manchuria for most of the war; nevertheless, he had this to say about his former enemy: "Whatever General Yamashita's transgressions of the laws and usages of war may have been, there can be no doubt that he was a most able and determined commander and a very tough fighter as his record both in Malaya and the Philippines will prove."

Apparently Percival shared some of Yamashita's views of the behavior of troops in wartime. He wrote: "It is a great pity that the Japanese commanders allowed and sometimes even ordered the atrocities which were committed by their officers and men. But that again may be due in some measure to the lack of time since their country emerged from its isolation. There was not enough time to absorb fully the accepted doctrines of civilisation."

What will be history's final verdict on Japan's greatest general? His record is a mixture of brilliance and bad luck.

He captured Singapore in the East's most decisive victory against the West. His success so frightened Japan's Premier that Tojo banished him to Manchuria for three years, in the middle of their country's most desperate war. Yamashita fought, on a shoestring, a spectacular year-long rear-guard action against General MacArthur, who was backed by all the mechanized might of America. He was hanged by what two United States Supreme Court judges called "legalized lynching."

But was it not the Japanese themselves who were responsible for his death? Was it not their indifference to human life, their archaic, inefficient chain of military command, their only partial integration into international civilization, their reckless gamble for conquest, which finally led this European-educated doctor's son to the scaffold one February morning?

Perhaps, as his Japanese biographer suggests, his execution in the Philippines was the best fate he could have expected. For what place would there be among the chromium, the neon signs, and the skyscrapers of Westernized postwar Japan for an out-of-date soldier who always began his day with a bow and a prayer, facing the Emperor?

He was an old-fashioned Oriental general, a product of his country and his time. Neither Japan nor the world will ever see his like again.

APPENDIXES

A Talk with Yamashita's Widow

Kamakura is a pretty seaside village tucked beside a small bay along the coast near Tokyo. On a narrow lane near the beach is a small wooden Japanese house surrounded by a tiny, parched lawn bordered by dwarf pine trees.

This was the home of Yamashita's widow. She greeted me in a gray kimono. Her white hair was carefully arranged, and she wore rimless spectacles. She looked like what she is—the daughter of one general and the widow of another.

Through the open sliding window, the shrill, musical cries of cicadas floated into the house. There was the faint scent of wood smoke in the air, and a delicate bell outside tinkled slightly in every small breeze.

She sat on a miniature overstuffed chair by a low lacquered table, her back to a small platform covered with straw matting, where she slept at night on a Japanese floor mattress. Overlooking this platform was a large oil painting of her husband in an ornate wooden frame. He was hatless and had a crew cut and a small mustache; he wore a green general's uniform and nineteen medals.

As Mrs. Yamashita talked, she moved a circular fan on which three green frogs were painted. She offered me glasses of Coca-Cola; this was followed by green tea in dark-brown bowls, and colored biscuits on green plates covered with a peach pattern.

Sipping her tea, she told me details of her husband's life. There was one aspect of it she was especially eager to discuss. "I have been very angry for a long time," she said, "about reports in the Western press that I pleaded with MacArthur to spare my husband's life. I never did this at any time. I would never have thought of doing it—and he would never have expected me to. He would have been very ashamed for me if I had done such a thing.

"I was not surprised when they decided to hang him. I thought it must come to that in the end. My husband was a man of great responsibility who would never have committed hara-kiri. He felt he could not die until all his men had been looked after.

"His death sentence was inevitable and natural because he was defeated. There is nothing surprising to the Japanese about this. In the old days, Japanese samurai who lost a battle automatically committed hara-kiri."

She paused to take a sip of tea, then continued thoughtfully. "I realize now that the Japanese mind is difficult for a foreigner to comprehend. Our national and religious background, founded upon the samurai spirit, must appear very strange to foreigners. I am afraid I have inherited from my father the severe samurai spirit of the past. That is why I would never appeal for mercy for my husband to General MacArthur."

She gazed at me sternly through her spectacles. Descended from the warrior nobles, about whom there are so many legends in her country, she was a survival from an almost vanished Japan.

Not very long ago, it was the custom that a samurai bride, on her wedding day, be given by her mother a small replica of a sword. This practice has died out in the last two generations, but it still lingered when Mrs. Yamashita married.

If anything went badly wrong with her marriage, it was the duty of the wife to kill herself with that tiny dagger.

The White Chrysanthemum

The Society of the White Chrysanthemum is an organization of the widows and relatives of executed Japanese war criminals. Its name was chosen with care: the Japanese regard the chrysanthemum as "a small, humble bloom which is easily overlooked."

Each year in May, the thousand members of the Society meet at the Yasukuni shrine, in Tokyo, to be greeted by the Emperor and Empress of Japan. Afterward, they are invited to the Imperial Palace for tea. This ceremony was initiated in 1959. Three years earlier, after gentle but persistent agitation, the members of the Society of the White Chrysanthemum were granted pensions from the State. This was in 1956, ten years after most of the war criminals had been condemned to death.

The Society has published a small, white-bound volume containing the last testaments, poems, essays, and other works written by the condemned as they awaited execution. Much of this material had been smuggled out by friends of the prisoners. Five thousand copies of this book have so far been distributed to schools and other organizations.

It was not only for pensions that the Society fought

so patiently. The members had a much more important aim: to have the names of their husbands and fathers inscribed in the memorial books at the Yasukuni shrine. On May 28, 1959, Emperor Hirohito ordered the white-robed Shinto priests to place the names of all dead Japanese war criminals on the sacred scrolls. After the ceremony, the Emperor and Empress prayed at a private shrine behind the main temple which is used only by bereaved relatives of soldiers who have died for their country. Then Hirohito addressed the White Chrysanthemums, saying: "I have a special appreciation for the families of our war criminals. I know what they have done for Japan. They were among our greatest leaders."

It was fitting that the ceremony should have been held at the Yasukuni shrine, the supreme citadel of the Japanese national mystique. It is not an ancient shrine—there are many much older—but its story tells the price Japan has paid to enter the modern world.

The shrine was founded a hundred years ago by Japan's most famous Emperor, Meiji, who first began to change his country from a medieval state into a great modern power. He ordered that the shrine be a place of worship where Japanese could always reverently remember those who had sacrificed their lives for their country. According to the Japanese belief, when the heroes' names were written in the books by the Shinto priests, they went straight to heaven to become gods.

The temple is surrounded by cherry trees and approached by long paved walks passing through torii, gates shaped like the Japanese character *torii*, which means gates. On the front of the building is the black outline of the Imperial chrysanthemum, a gift from the Emperor. Alongside it, a piece of paper flutters in the breeze. A poem by Meiji, Hirohito's grandfather, is written upon it.

The temple, like a large wooden canopy, is open on all sides. The large, straw-matted room is bare except for tassels hanging from the wooden beams. Through it can be seen the inner shrine, containing the names of the dead, guarded by two beautiful lamps like upturned tulips at the head of a flight of wooden steps.

Most countries have many memorials to their war dead, but Yasukuni is the only place of its kind in Japan. Every year, five million visitors come to pay homage. It is a place of pilgrimage for Japanese children, who march up to the temple carrying the flag of their school and stand gazing silently while relatives of those commemorated by the shrine clap hands to summon the spirits of the dead, toss some money into the box on the temple steps, and recite Shinto prayers in a low, rapid voice.

At the first enshrinement 3,588 names were placed on the scrolls. Now there are 2,500,000.

Among the first names to be placed there by the Emperor on behalf of the White Chrysanthemum Society, on May 28, 1959, was that of Tomoyuki Yamashita, General of the Imperial Japanese Army.

POEMS BY TOMOYUKI YAMASHITA
(Translated from the Japanese)

December 4, 1941: On Sailing for Hainan to Invade Malaya

On the day the sun shines with the moon
Our arrow leaves the bow.
It carries my spirit toward the enemy.
With me are a hundred million souls—
My people from the East—
On this day when the moon
And the sun both shine.

When He Heard of Japan's Surrender

The brassy sun burns down upon the earth—
An earth burnt black by battle.
From spring until the autumn leaf,
I have stood against the foe,
But not alone: with a million brave warriors
Serving their sacred Emperor.

Then suddenly I knew it all must end.
My soul overflowed with awe.
When the Emperor spoke to his people,
It knifed deep into my heart.

Yet, as I gaze into the sky,
How can I help the sorrow, the regret?
But I will be born seven times,
And once again will stand and fight

When my country wakes.

Before Giving Himself Up

My men have been gathered from the mountains
Like wild flowers.
Now it is my turn to go
And I go gladly.

After His Death Sentence

The world I knew is now a shameful place.
There will never come a better time
For me to die.

BIBLIOGRAPHY

Attiwill, Ken. *Fortress: The Story of the Siege and Fall of Singapore*. New York: Doubleday & Co., Inc., 1960; London: Frederick Muller, Ltd. (title: *The Singapore Story*), 1959.

Brown, Cecil. *Suez to Singapore*. New York: Random House, Inc., 1942.

Cannon, M. Hamlin. *The Return to the Philippines*. Washington: Department of the Army, Office of the Chief of Military History.

Chapman, F. Spencer. *The Jungle Is Neutral*. New York: W. W. Norton & Co., Inc.; London: Chatto & Windus, Ltd., 1949.

Churchill, Sir Winston. *The Second World War*. Six volumes. Boston: Houghton Mifflin Company; London: Cassell & Co., Ltd., 1948-1953.

Eichelberger, Robert Y. *Our Jungle Road to Tokyo*. New York: The Viking Press, Inc., 1950; London; Odhams Press, Ltd., 1951.

Gallagher, O'Dowd. *Action in the East*. New York: Doubleday & Co., Inc., 1942; London: George G. Harrap & Co., Ltd. (title: *Retreat in the East*), 1942.

Hunt, Frazier. *The Untold Story of Douglas MacArthur*. New York: Devin-Adair, 1954; London: Robert Hale, Ltd., 1955.

Krueger, Walter. *Down Under to Nippon*. Washington: Combat Forces Press, 1953.

Larteguy, Jean. (ed. and tr.) *Nihon Sembotsu Gakusei Shuki Henshū lin-kai. The Sun Goes Down: Last Letters from Japanese Suicide Pilots and Soldiers*. Tr. from the French by Nora Wydenbruck. London: William Kimber & Co., Ltd., 1956.

Morison, Samuel Eliot. *History of United States Naval Operations in World War II*. Vol. 12, *Leyte, June 1944–January 1945*. Vol. 13, *Liberation of the Philippines, Luzon, Mindanao, the Visayas, 1944-45*. Boston: Little, Brown and Co. (Atlantic Monthly Press); London: Oxford University Press, 1958-1959.

Owen, Frank. *The Fall of Singapore*. London: Michael Joseph, Ltd., 1960.

Percival, A. E. *The War in Malaya*. London: Eyre & Spottiswoode (Publishers), Ltd., 1949.

Reel, A. Frank. *The Case of General Yamashita*. Chicago: University of Chicago Press, 1949; London: Cambridge University Press, 1950.

Sastri, K. N., and K. D. Bhargava. *Official History of the Indian Armed Forces, Second World War*. Vol. 3, *Campaigns in South-east Asia: 1941-42*. Calcutta: Orient Longmans.

Stewart, Ian MacArthur. *History of the 2nd Argyll and Sutherland Highlanders*. London: Thomas Y. Nelson & Sons, 1947.

Storry, Richard. *A History of Modern Japan*. London: Penguin Books (Pelican A475), 1960.

Tsuji, Masanobu. *Singapore: The Japanese Version*. New York: St. Martin's Press, Inc., 1961.

Whitney, Courtney. *MacArthur: His Rendezvous with Destiny*. New York: Alfred A. Knopf, Inc.; London: McClelland & Stewart, Ltd., 1956.

Wigmore, Lionel. *The Japanese Thrust*. Sydney: Angus & Robertson, Ltd., 1958.

Willoughby, C. A., and J. R. Chamberlain. *MacArthur—1941-1951*. New York: McGraw-Hill, Inc., 1954; London: William Heinemann, Ltd., 1956.

Woodburn, Kirby, *et al. The War Against Japan*. Vol. 1, *The Loss of Singapore*. London: H. M. Stationery Office.

Woodward, C. Vann. *Battle for Leyte Gulf*. London & New York: The Macmillan Co., 1947.

The author consulted many other military histories, including those of the 6th Infantry Division, 37th Infantry Division, and 1st Cavalry Division, and many Japanese works not yet translated, including: F. Oki, *Yamashita Hobun;* K. Kurihara, *Doomed Army;* Hashimoto and Nakata, *The Last Moments of Ten Generals;* and Col. Hatori, *Operation Malaya*.

INDEX

Alor Star, 57, 63, 65
Anderson, Lt. Colonel, 72
Andoy, Rosalinda, 155
Asin River, 145
Asin valley, 148
Australia: Air Force, 57-58; invasion, 12-13, 42; troops at Singapore, 78-81
Australia, U.S.S., 130

Baguio, 127, 130, 132-33, 137, 141-43, 150-51
Bambang, 142-44
Bangkok, 48, 55
Batangas province, 156
Bayug, 118
Beightler, Maj. Gen. Robert S., 139
Bennett, Gen. Gordon, 84, 86
Bicycle troops, 60-62
Botanko, 96-97
Boxer Uprising, 18, 73
Breakneck Ridge, 112-13
British Army: 18th Div., 77; 11th Indian Div., 49, 52-53, 68; 22nd Australian Brig., 78, 82; 27th Australian Brig., 84; 2nd Indian Brig., 86; 44th Indian Brig., 84; 45th Indian Brig., 72; Argyll and Sutherland Highlanders, 74-75, 77; Dogras, 55; Frontier Force Rgt., 55; Hyderabad Rgt., 56; Malay Rgt., 86; Punjab Rgt., 59
Brooke-Popham, Air Chief Marshal Sir Robert, 50, 52-53, 57, 65

Bukit Timah, 84, 85, 88, 89
Burauen, 110, 117, 119-22
Buri airfield, 118-20
Burma, 12, 70, 98

Cagayan valley, 127, 141-42, 145, 151
Canberra, H.M.A.S., 106
Carpenter, Col. Alva, 154
Case of General Yamashita, The (Reel), 156, 160
Cebu, 122
China, 23, 29-30, 33, 42, 99
China Sea, 46, 49-50
Clarke, Col. Harry E., 158-59

Daily Express, London, 161
Down Under to Nippon (Krueger), 136
Dulag, 108, 117, 120
Duncan, Brigadier, 72

Endau River, 73, 76

Fall of Singapore, The (Owen), 80
Formosa, 45, 97, 103, 133-34, 142
Formosa Strait, 106, 109
Fort Canning, 88
Fort McKinley, 103-4, 134
Fort Santiago prison, 139, 158
Fukue, Lt. Gen. Shimpei, 122-23

Göring, Field Marshal, 33-34, 36
Gill, Maj. Gen. W. H., 150

Germany, 31-32, 34, 41
Geisha, 19, 25, 46, 102
Galang, Joaquin, 159

Haad'yai Junction, 48
Hainan Island, 42, 44, 46, 49, 51, 69
Halsey, Adm. William, 107
Hashimoto, Col. Hiroshi, 163
Heath, Gen. Sir Lewis, 52
Hendrix, Lt. Col. Walter, 167
Hirohito, Emperor, 25-29, 91, 180
Hiroshima, 18, 20, 43-44, 69
Hitler, Adolf, 13, 32-34
Homma, General, 101
Hong Kong, 42-43, 55
Honolulu, 106
Houston, U.S.S., 107

Iimura, Lt. Gen. Jo, 122
Ikatini, Colonel, 79
Imaye, Maj. General, 62, 77, 86, 92
Indochina, 44, 50-51, 57, 76, 125
Indonesia, 42, 43
Intramuros, 135, 138-40, 155
Ishikawa, Lt. Col. Kikuo, 163
Italy, 31, 34, 41
Iwabachi, Rear Adm. Sanji, 128, 134-37, 140, 153, 163

Japanese Air Force, 31, 38, 60, 78, 85, 92, 102, 123, 129; Fourth, 105, 127, 128, 165
Japanese Army: Kwantung Army, 99, 162; Singking Army Hq., 100; Southern Region Hq., 45, 51, 103, 121, 147, 150; 1st Army Grp., 96; 2nd Army Grp., 96; 14th Army Grp., 100, 122; 2nd Army, 122; 25th Army, 42, 66, 91; 35th Army, 104, 107, 114, 117, 121-22; 1st Div., 112, 114, 121; 5th Div., 43-44, 49, 54, 57, 59, 65-69; 71, 75-76, 80-81, 92; 10th Div.,
125; 16th Div., 107, 118-20; 18th Div., 43-44, 55, 57-58, 73, 76, 80-81; 19th Div., 125, 130; 23rd Div., 125, 130; 26th Div., 115, 118-20; 56th Div., 44, 70; 102nd Div., 122; 3rd Rgt., 23, 72, 76; 11th Rgt., 18, 20; Imperial Guards, 44, 53, 55, 62, 69, 71-73, 75-77, 83-85, 86-87, 91, 104
Japanese Navy, 50, 60, 85, 102, 106-7, 129, 134; 1st Fleet, 45; 31st Spec. Base Force, 128
Java, 65, 74, 84
Johore, 70, 76
Johore Causeway, 70, 74, 84
Johore Strait, 66, 73, 75, 78

Kamikaze, 128, 130-31
Keitel, Field Marshal, 33
Kelantan River, 43, 55, 57
Kerr, Maj. Robert N., 155, 165, 167-68
Key, Brigadier, 56
Keyes, Henry, 161
Kiangan, 144, 150
Kido, Marquis Koichi, 100
Kira, Maj. Gen. Goichi, 163
Koiso, Kuniaki, 99
Konoye, Prince Fumimaro, 31, 39
Korea, 130
Kota Bharu, 43, 45, 48, 56-58, 108; invasion, 55
Kra, Isthmus of, 43
Kranji River, 82, 83
Kru_ger, Gen. Walter, 108, 112, 114, 136, 138
Kuala Lumpur, 52, 67, 68, 70
Kuroda, Lt. Gen. Shijenori, 101-2, 126

Lapuz, Narciso, 157-59
Leyte Campaign, 101-24, 125; casualties, 123
Leyte Gulf, U.S. landing, 107-9, 118
Lingayen Gulf, 127, 130
Los Baños, 173

Luzon, 104-5, 107, 109, 113, 122; campaign, 125-52; U.S. landing, 130-31

MacArthur, Gen. Douglas, 12, 101, 108, 109, 111, 134, 136, 140-41, 147, 151, 154, 161, 167, 169, 172-73, 176
Makino, General, 107, 118
Malaya Campaign, 12, 41-93; casualties, 93
Manaki, Maj. General, 83, 86
Manchukuo, 24
Manchuria, 33, 96, 99, 133, 143, 151
Manchuria Incident, 23
Manchurian Army Group, 99
Manila, 11, 100, 103-5, 127-28; battle for, 134-40; casualties, 140
Manila Bay, 126, 135
Manila Cathedral, 139
Manila dam, 130
Manila Hotel, 136, 137-38
Matador, Plan, 49, 50, 52, 53, 59
McGrath, J. Howard, 169
Meiji, Emperor, 17, 18, 19, 180
Messerschmitts, 34
Milanes, Julietta, 155
Mindanao, 123
Mindoro, U.S. invasion, 122
Moon, Pvt. Harold H., 111
Muar River, 70-73, 85, 87, 92
Mukden, 20, 23
Murphy, Justice, 170-72
Mutaguchi, General, 76
Muto, Lt. Gen. Akira, 11, 104, 109, 113, 126, 129, 130, 143-44, 149, 163

Nagayama, General, 21
Nagayama, Hisako, 21
Nakasoni, Major, 43, 47-51, 54, 58
Newbiggin, Major General, 88
New Bilibid prison, 11, 151, 155, 159
New Guinea, 106

Newsweek, 161
New York Times, 155, 160, 163, 168
Nishimura, Lt. Gen. Takumo, 62, 69, 72-73, 76-77, 82-86, 104; hanged, 91
Noguchi, Colonel, 137
Nonaka, Captain, 25, 28

Okabayashi, Col. Junkichi, 114
Oki, Shuji, 175
Okinawa, 142
Okochi, Vice Adm. Denshichi, 127, 134, 162
Orders from Tokyo, 160
Ormoc, 111-12, 115-16, 118-20
Osugi Mura, 15

Palawan Island, 156-57, 165
Pattani, 43, 48-49, 59; invasion, 55
Pasig River, 134, 135
Parachute troops, 38, 117-19
Pearl Harbor, 23, 35, 41, 47, 55, 95, 109, 168
Penang, 57, 62, 63
Perak River, 63
Percival, Gen. Arthur, 48, 52, 57, 59, 71-72, 78, 84, 86-87, 89-90, 92, 97, 151, 175
Philippines, 42-43, 47, 55, 100; campaign, 101-52; Japanese forces, 105-6; casualties, 151-52; Catholics, 102-3; guerrilla activity, 103, 106, 121, 126, 156
Point Camau, 50
Port Arthur, 38
Prince of Wales, H.M.S., 51, 60
Prog, Mount, 146-50

Radar, 33, 35-36
R.A.F., 57, 58, 73, 74
Rayambugan Farm School, 145
Reel, A. Frank, 156, 160, 167
Repulse, H.M.S., 51, 60
Reynolds, Maj. Gen. R. B., 154, 156, 168
Ricarte, Gen. Artemio, 157-59

Romero, Biscumino, 159
"Rules Governing the Trial of War Criminals," 161
Russia, 12, 20, 24, 33, 35-37, 39, 96, 99; enters war, 148
Russo-Japanese War, 20, 96
Ryujo Maru, 47

Sadao, 59
Saigon, 45-46, 51, 58, 70, 73, 76, 114, 121-22, 128
Saipan, 98, 99, 106
San Francisco Radio, 114, 148
San José, 108
San Pablo, 118, 119
Santo Domingo, Church of, 139
Samah, 46
Sausage Island, 55
Sawada, General, 29, 30, 32
Seletar airfield, 57
Seoul, 29
Sho, Operations, 101
Sho One, Operation, 101
Siberia, 32, 134
Sierra Madre Mountains, 144, 146
Singapore, 12, 42, 44, 47-53, 55-57, 59, 62-63, 66, 70; battle for, 74-93; surrender, 88-90
Singapore Naval Base, 51, 57, 85
Singora, 43, 48-49, 52-54, 58-59, 63, 65, 92; invasion, 53
Slim River, 67-70
Smith, Robert Ross, 152
Sparnom, Capt. Norman, 160
"Spiderholes," 110, 112
Spitfires, 34
Stone, Chief Justice, 169-70
Straits Times, 88
Styer, Lt. Gen. Wilhelm D., 167
Suicide troops, 117-19
Sugita, Captain, 88, 91
Sumatra, 104, 109, 110
Supreme Court, Philippine, 167-68
Supreme Court, U.S., 155, 169-72, 176

Suzuki, Lt. Gen. Sosaku, 77, 90, 104-5, 107, 109, 112-14, 117, 119-23
Switzerland, 148

Tacloban, 101, 108, 111, 117, 120
Takeda, Prince, 45
Tengah airfield, 57, 84
Terauchi, Field Marshal Count Hisaichi, 29, 45, 91, 103-4, 110, 113, 122, 128, 130, 147, 149
Thailand, 43-44, 48-49, 52-53, 59, 125; army, 54; Japanese pact, 41, 54
Thomas, Gov. Sir Shenton, 88
Tojo, Hideki, 12-13, 21, 23, 31-32, 39, 41, 95-97, 99-102, 128, 133, 176
Tominaga, Lt. Gen., 127-28, 133-34
Tomochika, Gen. Yoshiharu, 119, 121
Toyoda, Adm. Soemu, 103
Tripartite Pact, 31, 41
Triumph in the Philippines (Smith), 152
Truman, President Harry S, 155, 173
Trumbull, Robert, 160
Tsuji, Col. Masanobu, 46, 66, 68-69, 83, 86

Umali, Panfilo, 156
Umezu, Gen. Yoshigiro, 99, 162
U.S. Army: Sixth Army, 108, 111, 136; 24th Div., 113; 32nd Div., 145, 150; 37th Div., 139; 77th Div., 115
U.S. Navy: Third Amphib. Force, 106; Third Fleet, 107; Seventh Fleet, 106

Vladivostok, 96

War in Malaya, The (Percival), 78, 81, 92
Watanabe, Colonel, 61

Wavell Gen. Sir Archibald, 65, 74, 84, 87

White Chrysanthemum, Society of, 179

Wild, Captain, 88

Yamamoto, Fleet Adm. Isoroku, 109

Yamashita, (Mrs.) Hisako, 29, 44, 97, 174; interview with, 177-78

Yamashita, Gen. Tomoyuki: birth, 15; "Great Cedar," 15-16; Kainan Middle School, 17-19; Central Military Academy, 19; War College, 20; marriage, 21; Bern, 21; Vienna, 21-22, 36; Chief of Military Affairs, 24; Young Officers' Revolt, 24-29; Korea, 29-30; Inspector General of Air Force, 31-32; Manchuria, 39, 41, 95-99, 176; Malaya campaign, 41-93; 25th Army, 42; 1st Army Grp., 96; 14th Army Grp., 100; Philippine campaign, 101-52; Baguio, 130-42; Bambang, 142-44; Kiangan, 144; Asin valley, 145; Mount Prog, 146-50; surrender, 151; New Bilibid prison, 11, 151; war-crimes charges, 154; war-crimes trial, 153-68; appeals, 169-73; execution, 175; poems by, 183-84

Yasukuni Shrine, 179-80

Yokosuka Naval Base, 35

Yokoyama, Lt. Gen. Shizuo, 127, 134, 136, 163

Young Officers' Revolt, 24-49

Zeros, 34, 73